COLORADO
Front Range
History Explorer

by

Nancy & David Muenker

Altitude Publishing

Colorado / Canadian Rockies / British Columbia

Publication Information

Altitude Publishing Canada Ltd.
The Canadian Rockies / British Columbia / Colorado
Head Office: 1500 Railway Avenue
Canmore, Alberta T1W 1P6
www.altitudepublishing.com
Copyright 2002 ©Nancy and David Muenker

Cataloging in Publication Data
Muenker, Nancy
Colorado Front Range History Explorer,
An Altitude SuperGuide
Includes index.
ISBN 1-55265-042-1
1. Historic sites—Front Range (Colo. and Wyo.)--Guidebooks. 2. Front Range (Colo. and Wyo.)--Guidebooks. I. Muenker, David, II. Title. III. Series: Altitude SuperGuide; Explore Colorado's Front Range
F782.F88M84 2002 917.88'60434 C2002-910149-2

Printed and bound in Western Canada by Friesens, Altona, Manitoba.

Altitude GreenTree Program
Altitude Publishing will plant twice as many trees as were used in the manufacturing of this product.

We acknowledge the financial support of the Government of Canada through the Book Publishing Industry Development Program (BPIDP) for our publishing activities.

Front Cover: Denver Civic Center Park;
Insets: Baby Doe Tabor and Buffalo Bill Cody
Back Cover: Garden of the Gods, Rock Ledge Ranch Historic Site

Project Development

Publisher	Stephen Hutchings
Associate Publishers	Dan Klinglesmith
	Patrick Soran
Concept/Art Direction	Stephen Hutchings
Design/Layout	Dan Klinglesmith
Editor	Dan Klinglesmith
Maps	Hermien Schuttenbeld
Index	Elizabeth Bell
Financial Management	Laurie Smith

Note from the Publisher
The world described in *Altitude SuperGuides* is a unique and fascinating place. It is a world filled with surprise and discovery, beauty and enjoyment, questions and answers. It is a world of people, cities, landscape, animals and wilderness as seen through the eyes of those who live in, work with, and care for this world. The process of describing this world is also a means of defining ourselves.

It is also a world of relationship, where people derive their meaning from a deep and abiding contact with the land—as well as from each other. And it is this sense of relationship that guides all of us at Altitude to ensure that these places continue to survive and evolve in the decades ahead.

Altitude SuperGuides are books intended to be used, as much as read. Like the world they describe, Altitude SuperGuides are evolving, adapting and growing. Please write to us with your comments and observations, and we will do our best to incorporate your ideas into future editions of these books.

Stephen Hutchings
Publisher

Contents

Introduction 5
  Highlights of History 8
  List of Historic Attractions 12
  Colorado Front Range Map 13

Greater Denver & Boulder 15
  Greater Denver 16
  Golden 27
  Boulder 30

Northern Front Range 35
  Greeley 36
  Longmont 38
  Ft. Collins 39
  Estes Park 41

Central Front Range 45
  Idaho Springs 47
  Georgetown / Silver Plume 49

Southern Front Range 53
  Colorado Springs 55
  Old Colorado City 57
  Manitou Springs 59
  Cripple Creek 61
  Pueblo 62
  Cañon City 64
  Trinidad 64

Summit County / Vail Valley 69
  Frisco 69
  Breckenridge 70
  Vail 75

Author & Photographer 80

Maps

Colorado Front Range 13
Greater Denver & Boulder 16
LoDo Walking Map 20
Pearl Street Historic District Walking Map . . 32
Northern Front Range 36
Ft. Collins Old Town Walking Map 40
Central Front Range 46

Georgetown Walking Map 48
Southern Front Range 54
Manitou Springs Walking Map 58
Cripple Creek Walking Map 60
Summit County / Vail Valley 70
Breckenridge Walking Map 72

How to use this Book

This book brims with descriptions of Front Range historic attractions, from Fort Collins to Trinidad. The Front Range encompasses the foothills and high plains that stretch north-south along the eastern flank of the Rocky Mountains. Because of their historic impact on the development of the Front Range, this guide also includes Bent's Fort, Leadville and sites in the mountain corridor that runs up Interstate 70 to Vail. The map on page 13 pinpoints the location of each attraction.

The book's five chapters present the historic sites by geographic region along the Front Range: Denver & Boulder, Northern Region, Central Region, Southern Region and Summit County / Vail Valley. In addition to a brief history of the region and descriptions of the attractions, each chapter includes a site location map. The chapters are color-coded as described below.

For a quick reference to the attractions, consult the chart and map on pages 12 and 13. They alphabetically list each site with its city location, basic admission information and page number.

The ***Colorado Front Range History Explorer*** is organized by the following color scheme.

Introduction . . . .   Central Front Range . . . .

Greater Denver & Boulder . . . .   Southern Front Range . . . .

Northern Front Range . . . .   Summit County / Vail Valley . . . . .

The Colorado Front Range

Docents reenact daily life chores at Bent's Old Fort National Historic Site near La Junta.

Early explorers branded the land abutting the Rocky Mountains "the Great American Desert." During his 1806 exploration of the Louisiana Purchase's southwestern boundary, Lieutenant Zebulon M. Pike described the plains as rolling waves without a speck of vegetable matter.

Stephen H. Long endorsed Pike's assessment on his 1820 expedition, decrying the region as uninhabitable by an agriculture-based society.

For another half-century, nomadic Indians continued traversing the Front Range, hunting game and summering in mountain valleys, with minimal encroachment by pioneers. European trappers and traders bartered with Indians and merchants at trading posts along Trapper's Trail, which stretched north-south from Fort Laramie to El Pueblo. The phenomenal profits of William Becknell's 1821

trade expedition to Santa Fe catapulted commerce between the United States and Mexico on the Santa Fe Trail. Bustling traffic on the trail's Mountain Route forged Bent's Fort into a major trading and supply center, and later led to the development of Trinidad. Until the mid-19th century, the Front Range served as a Native American homeland and a commercial crossroads.

Then gold was discovered. Rumors of the Russell brothers' find in 1858 at the confluence of Cherry Creek and the South Platte River spread like wildfire. The slogan "Pikes

Peak or Bust" propelled prospectors to the western landmark, 60 miles off course from the discovery. The gold craze spurted into the mountains as fortune seekers struck bonanzas in Chicago Creek, North Clear Creek, Blue River Valley and California Gulch. The towns of Idaho Springs, Black Hawk and Central City, Breckenridge and Leadville grew around them. Nascent cities along the Front Range—Denver, Golden, Boulder, Pueblo—flourished as they outfitted the mining camps with supplies and equipment.

In 1861, the U.S. Congress

Left: Ancient Native American trails crisscross Colorado's Front Range.

established the Colorado Territory. After a brief session in the territorial capital of Colorado City, the legislature moved the capital to Golden for five years, and then permanently to Denver. One of the legislature's first acts was establishment of a territorial prison. When offered the option of being the site for the penal institution or the university, Cañon City chose the prison.

Tensions mounted as prospectors and settlers advanced into Indian homelands. The tragic Sand Creek Massacre, in which U.S. soldiers attacked an encampment of Cheyenne and Arapaho, incited more hostilities. As a result, the federal government established Camp Collins and other military outposts to protect travelers on the overland trails and moved Indians onto distant reservations.

Concurrently, prospectors struck silver in Georgetown. The mountain town enjoyed a sustained boom for two decades. In nearby Black Hawk, Nathaniel Hill built the Front Range's first smelter, launching the era of hard rock mining.

The Denver Pacific and Kansas Pacific Railroads arrived in 1870, facilitating the transport of goods to mining camps and the growth of new communities along the Front Range. Within a decade, Colorado's population ballooned five-fold. Agricultural colonies brought the first great waves of settlers. Promoting the Union Colony of Colorado through Horace Greeley's *New York Tribune*, Nathan Meeker convinced hundreds to pull up their Eastern roots and settle on Colorado's dusty high plains. Other colonies settled Longmont and Fort Collins.

Convinced that a north-south railway would spur profitable development, railroad magnate General William Jackson Palmer built the Denver and Rio Grande Railroad. He founded Colorado Springs near Pikes Peak as a town for

the well to do. The lauded healing waters of Manitou Springs bubbled only four miles away.

By 1872, the railroad reached Pueblo. A decade later, steel rolled out of the town's Colorado Fuel & Iron Company. Area coal fields supplied the plant.

Colorado entered the Union as the 38th state in 1876, with Denver as its capital. The following year the University of Colorado held its first classes in Boulder. To obtain this educational institution, the city had to donate land and match the legislature's appropriation.

Although the 59ers had long since departed Colorado for more promising sites, a new wave of prospectors filled the void when Leadville miners tapped into rich veins of another precious metal—silver. The streets buzzed with rags-to-riches stories. Among the freshly-minted millionaires were "Unsinkable" Molly Brown and H.A.W. Tabor. When passage of the Sherman Silver Purchase Act underwrote the price of silver at more than $1 an ounce, prospecting and investing further intensified. Repeal of the act in 1893 dealt a crushing blow to the Silver Kings and much of Colorado's economy.

While Leadville collapsed, Cripple Creek boomed. Bob Womack discovered gold in Poverty Gulch in 1891, catapulting Colorado's greatest gold bonanza. Miners extracted more than an estimated half billion dollars worth of the precious metal.

By the early 20th century, Colorado Springs' tuberculosis sanitoriums became nationally renowned. The major Front Range cities boasted concert halls, universities and libraries. Tourism thrived around natural landscapes such as Pikes Peak, Garden of the Gods and Long's Peak. After naturalist Enos Mills' lifelong campaign, in 1915 the U.S. Congress established Rocky Mountain National Park.

Today, historic sites throughout the Colorado Front Range capture priceless cameos of the rich heritage that early residents bequeathed to us.

Top: El Pueblo Museum mural depicts the area's cultural diversity.
Right: The late 1800s Chambers home at Rock Ledge Ranch Historic

Highlights of History

Civic Center's bucking bronco and cowboy statue honors Denver's Wild West roots.

1803 The Louisiana Purchase adds a vast area of land to the United States, including most of what is now northern and eastern Colorado.

1806 Lt. Zebulon M. Pike reaches the site of present-day Pueblo and discovers "Grand Peak," later named for him, and the Royal Gorge.

1820 Major Stephen H. Long and a party of naturalists sight and name Long's Peak while exploring the South Platte River.

1821 The Santa Fe Trail opens to international commerce with the Mountain Route running along the Arkansas River.

1833 The Bent brothers and partner St. Vrain build Bent's Fort on the Santa Fe Trail. Fort Vasquez and other posts used by trappers and traders stretch along Trappers Trail.

1842 Jim Beckwourth and others establish El Pueblo trading post at the confluence of Fountain Creek and the Arkansas River.

1848 Under the Treaty of Guadalupe Hidalgo following the Mexican War, the United States acquires additional land in southern Colorado.

1858 William Green Russell's party discovers a small placer of gold near the confluence of South Platte River and Cherry Creek, precipitating a gold rush and the "Pikes Peak or Bust" slogan. Present-day Pueblo is founded as Fountain City.

1859 Prospectors pour into the mountains and discover gold along Chicago Creek, North Clear Creek and the Blue River. William N. Byers publishes the region's first newspaper, the *Rocky Mountain News.*

1860 Miners stampede to the rich gold discoveries at California Gulch, near present-day Leadville. The towns of Denver, named for the Kansas Territorial governor, James W. Denver, and Auraria formally merge. Don Felipe Baca and other New Mexican families found Trinidad.

1861 Congress establishes the Colorado Territory. William Gilpin becomes its first governor. During the first assembly, legislators select Colorado City as the territorial capital.

1862 After meeting in Colorado City, the legislature selects Golden as the new capital. Pioneers settle lands under the Homestead Act of 1862.

1864 The "Sand Creek Massacre," during which territorial troops killed 150 Cheyenne and Arapaho Indians at their encampment, sets off uprisings. Camp Collins is established to protect travelers on the Overland Trail. Colorado Seminary (now University of Denver) is founded.

1867 Territorial legislature selects Denver as the capital.

1868 Nathaniel Hill builds Colorado's first smelter in Black Hawk, launching the era of hard-rock mining.

1870 Rail transportation arrives in Colorado via the Denver and Pacific Railroad and the Kansas Pacific Railroad. Nathan Meeker founds the Union Colony at Greeley.

1871 General William J. Palmer builds the Denver and Rio Grande Railroad southward from Denver and founds Colorado Springs. The Colorado School of Mines is established at Golden. The territorial prison is erected at Cañon City. The Chicago-Colorado Company founds Longmont.

1872 The Larimer County Land Improvement Company establishes Fort Collins.

1874 Colorado College is founded at Colorado Springs. The legislature appropriates $15,000 for establishment of the University of Colorado at Boulder, provided that the city raise an equal sum.

1875 Lead carbonate ores, rich in silver, are found near the present site of Leadville.

1876 Colorado becomes the 38th State. John L. Routt is elected its first governor. Trinidad becomes incorporated.

1877 The University of Colorado holds its first classes at Boulder, with two teachers and 44 students. The St. Louis Smelting & Refining Company builds a smelter in Leadville, making profitable extraction of silver from the area's lead carbonate ores possible.

1878 Rich silver strikes in Leadville create numerous millionaires. Central City opera house opens.

1879 Colorado College of Agriculture and Mechanic Arts offers classes at Fort Collins. Utes slay Nathan C. Meeker, Indian Agent at the White River Agency, and several others.

1881 Ute tribes are banished to remote reservations.

1882 Pueblo processes steel in a plant later named Colorado Fuel and Iron Company.

1886 The Denver Union Stockyards are established and become the nation's largest receiving market for sheep.

1888 The Union Colony at Greeley completes a 900,000 acre irrigation project.

1890 Passage of the Sherman Silver Purchase Act raises the price of silver to more than $1 an ounce. The State Normal School (now the University of Northern Colorado) holds classes.

1891 Robert Womack's Cripple Creek gold discovery sets off Colorado's greatest gold boom. Pikes Peak cog railroad starts.

1893 Repeal of the Sherman Act crushes the silver mining industry, turning many "silver kings" into paupers.

1894 The State Capitol is completed at a cost of $2,500,000.

1900 The Denver Museum of Natural History, now the Denver Museum of Nature and Science, becomes incorporated.

1902 A beet sugar refinery is built at Fort Collins, starting a new agricultural industry.

1903 Mine, mill and smelter workers strike in several locations for better working conditions and higher wages.

1906 The United States Mint at Denver issues its first coins. The Western Stock Show Association holds the inaugural National Western Stock Show in a makeshift tent in Denver's stockyards.

1914 The state militia attacks a coal strikers' tent encampment near Trinidad, resulting in the "Ludlow Massacre" in which several strikers, women and children are killed.

1915 Congress creates Rocky Mountain National Park.

Colorado Front Range Historic Scenic Drives

Rides aboard the Ft. Collins Municipal Railway recall early days.

Many of the scenic byways that wind through the Front Range enchant travelers with historic locales and attractions bursting with lore. Stops amidst their splendid landscapes reveal the imprint of Indians, merchants, homesteaders, soldiers and countless other predecessors.

French-speaking fur trappers named the river that winds west of Fort Collins the **Cache la Poudre**. The scenic byway that parallels its wild waters bears the same name. As the story goes, a blustery snowstorm forced the trappers to turn back. To lighten their load, they stashed some of their supplies, including gun powder, "poudre," in a hole dug beside the river. The next spring they found their hiding place, or "cache," intact. Rocky Mountain bighorn sheep scale the cliffs behind the Arrowhead Lodge, a 1930s mountain resort for anglers and hikers. Designated a

National Historic District, the log structure now houses a visitor center whose exhibits describe area geology and history. At the drive's east terminus, the Avery House and Fort Collins Museum highlight the region's early travelers and settlers.

Peak to Peak scenic byway links the gold mining-era towns of Black Hawk and Central City with the eastern gateway of Rocky Mountain National Park, Estes Park. Every summer music fills the Central City Opera House. Amidst modern casinos, Black Hawk is creating Mountain City Historic Park to showcase its legacy through 19th-century structures. Winding through mountain forests and meadows, the highway passes Rollinsville, the starting point for a wagon road across the Continental Divide; Nederland, a community founded by Dutch silver mine investors; and Allenspark, once a homestead. The roadside cabin

of renowned naturalist Enos Mills fascinates visitors with memorabilia of the "father" of Rocky Mountain National Park. The Estes Park Area Historical Museum highlights the region's early explorers, homesteaders and vacationers.

Comprised of three historic travel routes, the **Gold Belt Tour** explores the dramatic area between Florissant and Florence, west of Colorado Springs. High Park Road, which traverses expansive ranch land, was the first route to connect the gold fields with the fertile Arkansas Valley. Phantom Canyon Road follows the rail bed of the Gold Belt Line, which transported more than 150 million dollars worth of gold ore from the boomtown of Cripple Creek. On Sunday excursions passengers rode either to dynamic Cripple Creek to shop or to Florence to picnic in peaceful fruit orchards. Shelf Road served as a toll stage route from the val-

Colorado Front Range Historic Scenic Drives

Costumed interpreters tend the farm at Rock Ledge Ranch Historic Site.

ley to the mining camps. Stagecoaches and freight wagons navigated the perilous, narrow road blasted out of the side walls of Fourmile Canyon. The routes converge near Cripple Creek and Victor, where travelers can explore vestiges of gold mining camps, tour the District Museum and descend 1,000 feet into the Mollie Kathleen Mine.

At the lofty elevation of 10,152 feet, Leadville, aka Cloud City, provides the historic highlight of the **Top of the Rockies** scenic byway. Abandoned mines, historic residences, museums and an opera house attest to an earlier era when silver polished the town to an opulent sheen. The route also passes the National Fish Hatchery, which since 1891 has stocked regional waters with trout, and the quaint silver-era village of Twin Lakes. At the top of Tennessee Pass, the Tenth Mountain Division Memorial commemorates the 5,000 ski and moun-

tain troops killed or wounded in World War II. Their former training site, Camp Hale, lies in peaceful Pando Valley.

In southeastern Colorado, the **Santa Fe Trail** scenic drive traces the 19th-century commercial route over which freight wagons teeming with profitable goods lumbered and groaned. Today's travelers can visit former trail supply centers that provided safe havens to weary wayfarers. At Bent's Old Fort National Historic Site, interpreters representing fur traders, Native Americans and freighters re-enact the bustling trade depot's daily activities. The Mountain Route coursed through the center of Trinidad, now the Corazon de Trinidad National Historic District. Two stately historic residences, the Baca House and Bloom Mansion, tower alongside the former trail. Visits to the Trinidad History Museum include colorful narrated tours of these properties.

From Trinidad, the **Highway of Legends** scenic drive loops northwest, rising from arid plains over Cuchara Pass to the Spanish Peaks, which Native Americans called the "Breasts of Earth," the wellspring of life. Ebony mounds of slag mark the entrance to Cokedale, built in 1907 as a model mining camp. Townsfolk continue to reside in its tiny, square stucco houses. Signs indicate the bathhouse, mercantile store and other former company buildings. Farm communities founded by Hispanic families in the 1860s hug the Purgatoire River while ranches cover Cuchara Valley. Established as a fort, La Veta has evolved into an art community. The Devil's Staircase, Dakota Wall and other bizarre formations have inspired countless legends, from tales of lost gold mines to giant gods.

Colorado Front Range Historic Attractions

ATTRACTION	LOCATION	ADMISSION	PAGE #	MAP #
Argo Gold Mill-Mine-Museum	Idaho Springs	Admission Charged	47	28
Astor House Museum	Golden	Admission Charged	28	11
Avery House	Fort Collins	Free	39	23
Bent's Old Fort National Historic Site	La Junta	Admission Charged	67	48
Black American West Museum & Heritage Center	Denver	Admission Charged	24	8
Breckenridge Historic District Walking Tour	Breckenridge	Admission Charged	70	50
Briggle House and Milne Cabin	Breckenridge	Admission Charged	70	50
Buffalo Bill Memorial Museum and Grave	Golden	Admission Charged	30	15
Byers-Evans House Museum	Denver	Admission Charged	17	2
Centennial Village Museum	Greeley	Admission Charged	38	19
Clear Creek History Park	Golden	Admission Charged	29	14
Colorado State Capitol	Denver	Free	17	3
Colorado History Museum	Denver	Admission Charged	16	1
Colorado Railroad Museum	Golden	Admission Charged	29	13
Colorado Ski Museum/Colorado Ski Hall of Fame	Vail	Admission Charged	75	54
Colorado Springs Pioneers Museum	Colorado Springs	Free	55	34
Cripple Creek District Museum	Cripple Creek	Admission Charged	62	42
Edgar Experimental Mine	Idaho Springs	Admission Charged	49	30
Edwin Carter Museum	Breckenridge	Admission Charged	71	51
El Pueblo Museum	Pueblo	Admission Charged	63	43
Enos Mills Cabin	Estes Park	Donations Accepted	42	25
Estes Park Area Historical Museum	Estes Park	Admission Charged	41	24
Fort Collins Museum	Fort Collins	Free; Donations Accepted	39	22
Fort Collins Old Town	Fort Collins	Free	39	21
Fort Vasquez Museum	Platteville	Free	35	17
Four Mile Historic Park	Denver	Admission Charged	24	9
Frisco Historic Park	Frisco	Free	69	49
Georgetown Loop Railroad	Georgetown	Admission Charged	51	33
Golden Pioneer Museum	Golden	Free	28	12
Hamill House Museum	Georgetown	Admission Charged	50	32
Healy House and Dexter Cabin Museum	Leadville	Admission Charged	77	55
Hiwan Homestead Museum	Evergreen	Free	45	27
Hotel de Paris Museum	Georgetown	Admission Charged	51	31
Larimer Square	Denver	Free	19	7
Littleton Historical Museum	Littleton	Free	26	10
Lomax Placer Gulch	Breckenridge	Admission Charged	71	52
Longmont Museum	Longmont	Free	39	20
Lower Downtown	Denver	Free	19	6
MacGregor Ranch Museum	Estes Park	Donations Accepted	42	26
McAllister House Museum	Colorado Springs	Admission Charged	56	35
Meeker Home Museum	Greeley	Free	37	18
Miramont Castle Museum	Manitou Springs	Admission Charged	61	39
Molly Brown House	Denver	Admission Charged	18	4
Mollie Kathleen Gold Mine	Cripple Creek	Admission Charged	62	41
Museum of Colorado Prisons	Cañon City	Admission Charged	64	46
National Mining Hall of Fame & Museum	Leadville	Admission Charged	77	56
Ninth Street Historic Park	Denver	Free	18	5
Old Colorado City History Center	Colorado Springs	Free	59	38
Pearl Street Historic District	Boulder	Free	31	16
Phoenix Gold Mine	Idaho Springs	Admission Charged	47	29
Pikes Peak Cog Railway	Manitou Springs	Admission Charged	61	40
Pueblo County Historical Museum	Pueblo	Free	63	45
Rock Ledge Ranch Historic Site	Colorado Springs	Admission Charged	57	37
Rosemount Museum	Pueblo	Admission Charged	63	44
Trinidad History Museum	Trinidad	Admission Charged	65	47
Washington Gold Mine	Breckenridge	Admission Charged	75	53
Western Museum of Mining & Industry	Colorado Springs	Admission Charged	56	36

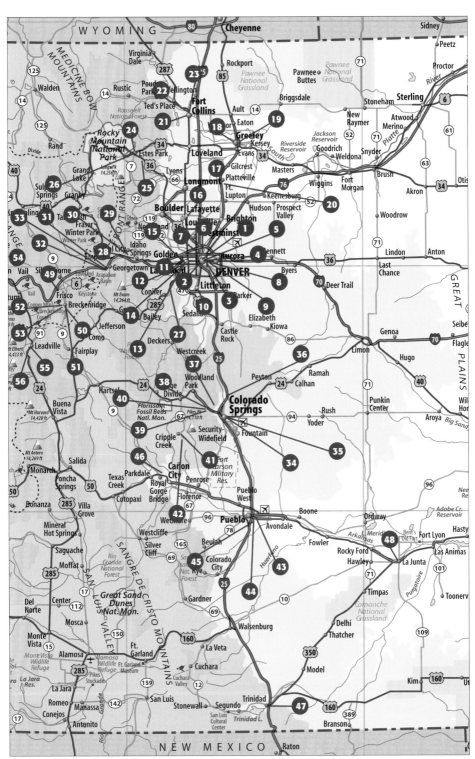

Greater Denver & Boulder

Seen from Denver's City Park, Mount Evans rises majestically behind the onetime City Park boathouse.

Gold! The news spread eastward like prairie fire when in 1858 the Russell brothers discovered the precious metal at Cherry Creek. Fortune seekers known as the 59ers streamed to the Rocky Mountains. The Russells and their party of Georgians named their camp Auraria.

Across the creek, another group of prospectors established a settlement called St. Charles. That name, however, lasted scarcely a year. Before its founders managed to register their township, General William H. Larimer, Jr., laid claim to the site, naming it Denver City, after James Denver, territorial governor of Kansas. The primary commercial area ran down the general's namesake, Larimer Street. Denver City formally united in 1860 during a moonlit ceremony on the bridge spanning Cherry Creek.

Concurrently, other towns sprouted on the Front Range. Golden took root at the mouth of Clear Creek Canyon where Thomas L. Golden had camped. Farther north, Boulder formed at the base of the Flatirons within a month of a nearby gold strike. Farmers and ranchers gravitated to its fertile valley.

As thousands of eager miners and homesteaders poured in, ramshackle settlements vied to lead the burgeoning region. Golden served as the second capital of the Colorado Territory, until 1867 when Denver leaders won the designation for their community.

The arrival of the railroad in 1870 secured Denver's position as the territory's commercial, financial and political hub. Wholesalers and merchandisers established businesses around Union Station. Attracted by a larger labor force and economies of scale, smelters moved from mining towns into the city.

Additional discoveries of gold and silver in Colorado's mountains during the late 1800s enriched Denver. The resultant influx of wealth bolstered development of elegant hotels, theaters, residences and boulevards, earning the

Left: Gold glimmers atop the Colorado State Capitol Building in Denver.

capital the title "Queen City of the Plains."

By 1900, the creekside settlement, whose population had stagnated at 5,000 souls during its first 20 years, blossomed into a thriving metropolis of 134,000.

Greater Denver

1. Colorado History Museum

1300 Broadway
(303) 866-3682
Open daily
Admission charged
Located at 13th Avenue and Broadway in downtown Denver

An intriguing mural of scenes and personages graces the face of the Colorado History Museum, hinting at the treasures that lie within. In the museum's foyer, a floor-to-ceiling display behind a curved glass wall exhibits an array of items that characterized life in early Colorado. Angora chaps, saddles and rifles counterpoint bonnets, upholstered chairs and elegant clocks. In the center, an exquisite wood-framed mirror captures visitors' images inside this historic collage.

From teepees and covered wagons to cowboy saddles and mining tools, gallery artifacts feature the lifestyles, equipment and events that contributed to the state's development. A large diorama depicts early Denver as it settled along Cherry Creek.

On a long wall, the Colorado Chronicle narrates 150 years of state history with interpretive panels, photos and maps. A Colorado timeline notes momentous state events

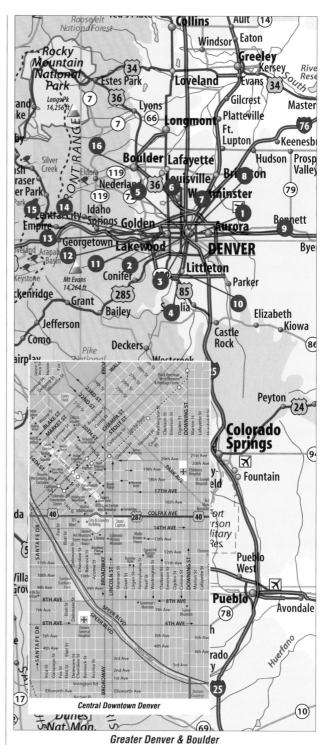

Central Downtown Denver

Greater Denver & Boulder

while a U.S. and international timeline places them within national and world context. For example, the year that Colorado won statehood and Denver became the state capital—1876—Alexander Graham Bell patented the telephone, Mark Twain published Tom Sawyer, the National Baseball League formed, Porfirio Diaz became dictator of Mexico and the United States' worst grasshopper plague ended.

2. Byers-Evans House Museum

1310 Bannock Street
(303) 620-4933
Open daily except Mondays and holidays
Admission charged

Located at 13th Avenue and Bannock Street downtown.

The Byers-Evans House Museum embraces the lives of two distinguished Colorado families. William N. Byers, the publisher of Denver's first newspaper, the *Rocky Mountain News*, built the house in 1883. Six years later, he sold his residence to William Gray Evans, son of Colorado's second territorial governor, John Evans, and president of the Denver Tramway Company. Members of the Evans family lived here for another 95 years. Restored to the 1912-1924 period, the house contains many original furnishings and distinctive features, such as fireplace tiles representing Aesop's fables which served as visual aids for story-telling.

3. Colorado State Capitol

200 East Colfax Avenue
(303) 866-2604
Open Monday through Friday
Free, hourly tours
Located at the corner of Colfax Avenue and Lincoln Street in downtown Denver

Gold glimmers atop the state capitol, thanks to Colorado miners who donated 200 ounces of the precious metal to replace the original copper cap. On the west entrance, the 18th step measures exactly 5,280 feet above sea level, the dimension that gave the Mile High City its moniker. Inside, priceless Colorado rose onyx marble, found nowhere else in the world, wainscots the building's walls. Marble from the same quarry that supplied lustrous stone for the Lincoln Memorial forms floors and

Denver / Boulder Recommendations

Tour the State Capitol to view the 16 Hall of Fame stained glass portraits of Colorado's early leaders.

Climb aboard a steam locomotive and examine memorabilia in a replica 1880s depot at the Colorado Railroad Museum.

Chat with 1800s homesteaders, farmers and blacksmiths while strolling through the farmsteads at Littleton Historical Museum.

Hear the rags-to-riches life tale of Margaret Tobin, who became an international heroine after the Titanic disaster, at the Molly Brown House.

Saunter through the serene setting of Chautauqua Park, whose annual programs have enhanced literary, oratory and music appreciation for more than 100 years.

Denver's Mother of Charities

When Frances Wisebart Jacobs moved to booming Denver in the 1870s, the plight of its underclass deeply concerned her. Abandoned children, homeless battered women and indigent tuberculosis sufferers helplessly roamed the mean streets. Leaving the safety of her parlor, she delivered food, medicine and solace to the slums' downtrodden. Directing local charities, she helped raise funds for shelters and free clinics. In 1887, she and four religious leaders successfully fused Denver's two dozen private charities into a unified federation, the Charity Organization Society—forerunner of the United Way. Later she helped establish the Jewish Hospital Association to build a hospital specializing in tuberculosis treatment. It evolved into the National Jewish Center for Immunology and Respiratory Medicine. Frances Jacobs (1843-1892) is the only woman enshrined in the capitol dome's Colorado Hall of Fame.

FRANCES JACOBS

stairs. Illustrating the state's story in picture and verse, murals on the first floor rotunda walls stress the importance of water to the West's development. From the third floor, 93 steps wind up to the dome balcony, where visitors can behold the Colorado Hall of Fame's 16 stained glass portraits (may be temporarily closed). Among those honored for their contribution to the state's initial growth and development are Kit Carson and Chief Ouray. Outside, the observation deck reveals sweeping views of downtown and the Rocky Mountains.

4. Molly Brown House

1340 Pennsylvania Street
(303) 832-4092
Open daily June through August, closed Mondays September through May
Admission charged
Three blocks east of the State Capitol and 1.5 blocks south of Colfax Avenue

On tours of the Molly Brown House, docents tell the rags to riches story of Margaret Tobin, born into a poor working class family in Hannibal, Missouri. Like thousands of other dreamers, she and her husband, J.J. Brown, sought mineral riches in Leadville, Colorado. Unlike most other miners, though, J.J. struck gold, making them millionaires. Now wealthy, they traveled to Europe and Asia and threw

Molly Brown and the Molly Brown House.

lavish parties for Denver's high society in their lavastone residence. After Molly's fateful journey aboard the Titanic, she gained world renown for her selfless efforts assisting immigrant women and children survivors. Likewise, she used her money and fame to benefit women's suffrage, local Catholic charities and efforts to reform maritime law. Today, the restored house interprets the style of an upper middle-class home of the late 19th and early 20th centuries. While light beams through the stairwell's original stained glass windows, the foyer glimmers with gold-painted

anaglypta, pressed paper wall covering. The painted dining room ceiling resembles a conservatory dome. Among the decorative objects that belonged to Molly is the Blackmoor statue in the entryway, which "received" visitors calling cards.

5. Ninth Street Historic Park

1020 to 1068 Ninth Street
Open year-round for self-guided walking tours
Free
West of Speer Blvd between Champa and Curtis Streets, on downtown Denver's Auraria Campus

Fourteen structures in Ninth Street Historic Park represent Denver's middle class housing of the late 19th-century. This restored residential block sits in the heart of the Auraria Campus, the former townsite on the west banks of Cherry Creek that the Russell brothers staked out in 1858. Inflated accounts of their small gold strike spurred settlement of this flourishing community, primarily by German and Irish families. Several of the park's buildings are territorial style, built before Colorado became a state. Only two cottages sport frame construction because after the devastating fire of 1863, an ordinance required the use of brick. Today local residents and businesses occupy these restored dwellings.

6. Lower Downtown (LoDo)
14th to 20th Streets and Larimer to Wynkoop Streets
Self-guided walking tours
Free
Northern section of downtown Denver

7. Larimer Square
Larimer Street at 14th Street
Self-guided walking tours
Free
Located on Larimer Street between 14th and 15th Streets in downtown Denver

Lower Downtown, or LoDo, encompasses 25 thriving residential and commercial blocks in the northern section of downtown Denver. Within it lies the city's original thoroughfare, Larimer Street. Denver's first bank, bookstore, photography studio and dry goods store sprang up on what is now the 1400 block. Eventually, stately stone structures replaced humble cabins and one-story, false-front stores. New enterprises flourished upon the arrival of the railroad in 1870. While development of a streetcar system shifted retail trade uptown, wholesale businesses rimmed the rail yards. Four downtown train stations served the dozens of railroads serving Denver until the network became consolidated into a central location, the Union Depot. Construction of huge, multi-story warehouses spiraled. Elegant hostelries, such as The Oxford Hotel, accommodated businessmen and other travelers.

The area's fortunes ebbed and flowed until the end of World War II when LoDo began to suffer a steady decline. New warehouse design and technology outmoded its facilities. As companies increasingly transported freight over the new interstate highway system, the number of trains arriving daily at the station decreased to as few as one. LoDo degenerated into a district of flophouses and abandoned buildings.

In the 1960s, however, Denver's oldest street soared to its rightful stature when real estate developer Dana Crawford led a renovation campaign. The successful rejuvenation of the 1400 block into Larimer Square resulted in its designation in 1973 as the city's first historic district. Emboldened by this accomplishment, other urban pioneers began to renovate buildings in LoDo. Professional offices, design centers, art galleries, restaurants and upscale lofts soon occupied

Denver's Grand Historic Hotels

The Oxford Hotel

The Brown Palace Hotel

Denver's two centenarian hotels opened within a year of each other. Located near bustling Union Station in Lower Downtown, The Oxford Hotel (303) 628-5400 awed its first guests with steam heat, gas and electric lighting, and bathrooms on each floor. Its elegant dining room served such delicacies as lamb kidneys and German asparagus on Haviland china. The following year, The Brown Palace (303) 297-3111, debuted with an eight-story Italian Renaissance atrium lobby lined in Mexican white onyx. Occupying a triangular plot at Broadway, Tremont and 17th Streets, the hotel continually hosts presidents, royalty and other luminaries. Both properties are listed on the Register of National Historic Places.

LoDo Walking Map

1. St. Elmo Hotel, 1433 17th Street
Located only two blocks from Union Station, this modest hotel catered to railway workers and passengers seeking moderate-priced lodging. Ornate features include a cornice box with frieze and brackets.

2. Barney Ford Building, 1514 Blake Street
An African-American pioneer who escaped from slavery, prominent politician and astute businessman, Barney Ford constructed this building for his People's Restaurant. He had a barber shop and hair salon in the basement and a saloon on the second floor. The facade's four decorative columns may be originals.

3. Merchandise Mart, 1863 Wazee Street
An Art Deco design in brick with terra-cotta accents distinguishes this structure. Originally built as a multi-tenant merchandise mart, it presently houses loft condominiums.

13. Chester S. Morey Mercantile Building, 1528 16th Street
Presently home to the downtown location of the Tattered Cover Book Store, this structure was once an elegantly appointed warehouse that also housed showrooms and corporate offices. Railcar loading docks and retail storefronts lined the double-wide alley off 16th Street.

12. Barteldes, Hartig Building, 1600 Wynkoop Street
Featuring textured brickwork, this building first served as a seed, fruit and produce warehouse. The main entrance was located on the second story where a bridge walkway connected it to the former 16th Street Viaduct, which stretched from Wazee Street across the Platte River.

11. Union Station, 17th and Wynkoop Streets
Opened in 1881, the Denver Union Depot consolidated the train stations that served the city's numerous railroads. Today, only the building wings date to the original Romanesque structure. Destroyed by fire, the main section was rebuilt in the 1890s. Besides today's cross-country travelers, Union Station serves Ski Train day-trippers to Winter Park Resort.

LoDo Walking Map

4. Oxford Hotel, 1612 17th Street

A lavish interior, luxurious amenities and proximity to Union Station made this hotel a grand success in 1891. The Cruise Room, its 1930s Art Deco bar, has its own listing in the National Register of Historic Places. Major restoration of the hotel recaptured its historic charm for today's guests.

5. Sugar Building, 1530 16th Street

This 1906 structure housed the administrative offices of the Great Western Sugar Company, formed by the merger of six small independent sugar beet factories. Geometric and stylized foliage terra-cotta decorations accent the exterior walls.

6. Henry Lee Building, 1545 Wazee St.

Built by a legislator and agriculturist instrumental in developing Denver's park system, the building first served as a warehouse. Later, it housed a spice mill, a peanut butter factory and coffee-roasting facilities.

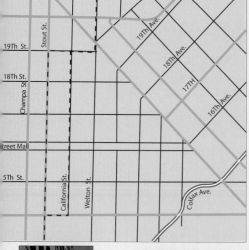

7. 15th / Wazee Street
1600-1610 15th Street

This 19th-century brick commercial structure with an angled corner entrance actually contains three buildings. Among its first occupants was the Bon Ton Saloon. The Wazee Supper Club has operated here since 1954.

10. Denver City Railway Building, 1635 17th St.

This building served as the Denver City Railway Company's main car barn for its horsecar lines, which ran from 1871 until electric and cable car networks replaced them in the 1890s.

9. Icehouse, 1801 Wynkoop Street

For nearly 80 years, this structure produced butter, cheese, cream and other dairy supplies, first as the Littleton Creamery and then as the Beatrice Company. Distinctive polychromatic brickwork with alternating bands of dark red, beige and light pink bricks pattern the exterior walls.

8. Elephant Corral, 1444 Wazee Street

A large corral and a hewn cottonwood log building with canvas roof were erected on this site when Denver was founded. Emigrants traded, bought and sold livestock at the coral, but not elephants. The reason for the corral's name is open to speculation. A brick warehouse, which still stands, replaced the frame building after the great fire of 1863.

A block of stately late 19th-century structures forms Denver's first historic district, Larimer Square. Some of the secrets whispered inside the buildings' red brick walls have survived the years, embellishing their facades with lore. Walking tour brochures (available at the square's information booth in Noel Park and at the Denver Metro

Convention & Visitors Bureau) help relate their stories. The second-floor dance hall in Lincoln Hall, for example, was originally suspended on springs. And Gahan's Saloon, the favorite watering hole for politicians, police offi-
cers and city hall reporters, reportedly harbored Denver's hottest speakeasy during Prohibition.

the old warehouses. In March 1988, Denver declared Lower Downtown a historic district. The construction of Coors Field baseball stadium spurred further renovation. Walking tours and interpretive plaques on exterior walls of cafes, galleries and condominium residences place these buildings in historic perspective. As in the late 1800s, today LoDo is where it's happening.

8. The Black American West Museum & Heritage Center

3091 California Street
(303) 292-2566
Open daily May through September; Wednesday through Sunday October through April; closed major holidays
Admission charged
Located in the Five Points Neighborhood across the street from the 30th & Downing light rail station

African Americans played an integral role in settling and shaping the American West, yet few history books adequately chronicle their contribution. With special emphasis on Colorado and early Denver, The Black American West Museum & Heritage Center recounts many of the untold stories. Black families, for example, came West in covered wagons and gained land ownership under the race-blind Homestead Act of 1862. Historic photographs and memorabilia throughout the museum portray the sundry occupations of African Americans in the West, among them fur trappers, homesteaders, ranchers, cowboys, bronco busters and miners. A room

exhibiting a doctor's examination table and medical paraphernalia honor the work of Justina Ford, MD. Undaunted by the racism that denied her hospital privileges for many years, she tirelessly brought medical services to Denver's disadvantaged. During half a century, she delivered more than 7,000 babies. Her residence now houses the museum.

9. Four Mile Historic Park

715 South Forest Street
(303) 399-1859
Open April through September and for special events
Admission charged
Located south of Leetsdale Avenue between Cherry Street and Monaco Boulevard.

As gold-seekers stampeded to Colorado in the early 1860s, astute entrepreneurs followed closely behind, establishing critical services such as transportation and lodging. One of them was a widow named Mary Cawker. Four miles outside Denver, at what is now Four Mile Historic Park, she turned her frontier home on

Black Cowboys and Buffalo Soldiers

Nat Love, a.k.a. Deadwood Dick

Nearly a third of the cowboys in the West were African Americans. Besides roping, riding and branding, they took on the dangerous tasks of testing swollen streams and breaking the toughest horses. Racism prevented all but a few from rising from cow-

hand to trail boss, but paradoxically it also created unique tasks, such as carrying the payroll. Thieves, trail bosses surmised, would not expect a black to be entrusted with valuables. Among the notable cowboys was Nat Love, an acclaimed rodeo performer and trick shot artist.

While cowboys drove cattle to frontier towns, black soldiers helped expand the West by fighting and displacing Native Americans. In the 1860s, Congress provided for four regular army infantry regiments and two cavalry regiments composed exclusively of black enlisted men. From surplus equipment to cast-off horses, they received the worst supplies. Moreover, African American units often shouldered combat duties far out of proportion to their numbers. Their valor, though, did not go unrecognized by their foes—Native Americans named them the "Buffalo Soldiers."

A shopkeeper greets visitors with old-time wares at Denver's Four Mile House.

the bustling Cherokee Trail into a wayside tavern, inn and stagecoach stop. Her business flourished. The flood of 1864, however, dampened her entrepreneurial spirit. Levi and Millie Booth of Wisconsin purchased her 160-acre farm and continued operating the stagecoach stop and tavern until the railroad arrived in Denver. The Booth family eventually added 500 acres of ranch land and became agricultural leaders in the region.

Today, Four Mile Historic Park occupies 11 acres of the original site. The living history farmstead re-creates frontier life from 1859 to 1883. Authentically dressed guides lead tours through Four Mile House, the oldest standing structure in Denver. Special events feature crafts, folklore and music of that time. On weekends, dust swirls above a segment of the old Cherokee Trail as modern-day passengers sample the rigors of stagecoach travel.

Critters and Spurs

The National Western Stock Show had humble beginnings. On January 29, 1906, a tent in Denver's stockyards hosted its inaugural. Today an 80-acre complex of multiple buildings showcases its exhibits and events. Except for one year when foot and mouth disease forced its cancellation, the show has happened every January.

Throughout the two-week event, some 600,000 people watch judging in the show rings, hear the auctioneer's warp-speed babble, pet baby critters in the children's ranch land and cheer on daring bull riders at the rodeo.

Livestock competition, however, is the focus. Contestants show quarter horses, hogs, steers and other animals for coveted awards. In one case, the owner's desire to win outweighed honesty. His entry, Big Mac, which in fact was a Charolais-Charolais cross breed he dyed black, won the Junior Angus Grand Champion Steer competition. Following up on contestants' suspicions, an investigation discovered the ruse and Big Mac lost his title.

Why hold the show in the dead of winter? According to one National Western officer, the month was chosen primarily to accommodate the stockmen. Leaving their ranches in January is less difficult. Visitors don't need to consult weather reports during the stock show. Invariably, it seems, the temperature is frigid.

10. Littleton Historical Museum

6028 South Gallup Street
(303) 795-3950
Open year-round Tuesday through Sunday, except holidays
Free
Located south of Littleton Blvd. between South Broadway and South Santa Fe Drive

South of Denver, farmhands plow fields and women stir stews on open fires at the Littleton Historical Museum. This living history museum in the South Platte Valley portrays both the simple pleasures and daily drudgery of early settlers on an 1860s farm and the improved conditions on an 1890s farm. In the McBroom Cabin, a costumed homesteader tells about her family's journey west and how neighbors helped build their one-room log home in two weeks. Keeping a watchful eye on the cast iron pots cooking a cobbler and the noon meal, she washes dishes in a small basin with harsh soap and a rag. Outside, piglets wallow in sties, cows low in a paddock and draft horses clop down a dirt road. Beyond the fields, a schoolmarm teaches the ABCs in Littleton's first schoolhouse. Wallpaper, lace curtains, fine furniture and an array of kitchen implements in the Bemis 1890s residence accentuate how rail transportation of goods made homes more comfortable and attractive. The tantalizing aroma of cookies freshly baked in the kitchen's large stove wafts throughout the house. Plinks of metal against anvil resound in a nearby wood

shed. Inside, a blacksmith hammers horseshoes and hinges. From nails to crowbars, he supplies the homesteads' iron implements. The farms' drama unfolds throughout the seasons. In spring, workers plant seeds in tilled fields while young calves and lambs romp. Crops stretch skyward under the hot summer sun. In autumn, farmhands harvest golden pumpkins, gather honey from the beehives and brew apple cider. When snow blankets the pastures and ice glazes Ketring Lake, evergreen garlands and glowing candles brighten the houses.

Between the two living history farms, the museum building displays priceless items from its impressive collection

Fun Historic Facts about Denver

• **When a regular customer** ordered his standard glass of cream charged with soda before the morning cream delivery, Denver restaurateur Otto Baur substituted ice cream for the cream. Thus, in 1871, the ice cream soda was born.

• **Copper originally** covered the dome of the capitol. Colorado miners donated 200 ounces of gold to ensure that the state's primary metal would top the structure.

• **The nation's first** juvenile court was started in Denver in 1903 by Judge Ben B. Lindsey. The court became a model for other cities around the world.

• **Denverite John A. Valentine** created the first flowers-by-wire service when, in 1910, he persuaded 14 other florists to join him in organizing the Florists' Telegraph Delivery Association. Later, the name changed to Florists' Transworld Delivery Association (FTD).

• **While experimenting** with various toppings, Humpty Dumpty Drive-in owner, Louis Ballast, slapped a piece of American cheese on a sizzling hamburger. Pleased with the tasty result, he named it the "cheeseburger" and registered his creation with the State of Colorado on March 5, 1935.

• **The Denver Boot**—a wheel clamp that immobilizes cars whose owners have unpaid traffic violations—was invented in 1944 to replace impoundment. Cities throughout the United States now use the Denver Boot.

• **Several famous authors,** actors, political leaders and other luminaries attended Denver high schools. Among them were Secretary of State Madeleine Albright; playwright Mary Coyle Chase, who won the 1945 Pulitzer Prize for "Harvey"; silent film star Douglas Fairbanks; Israeli Prime Minister Golda Meier; "Gone With the Wind" actress Hattie McDaniel, the first black to win an Academy Award; and Apollo XIII astronaut John L. "Jack" Swigert, Jr.

• **When the Colorado Rockies** baseball team took the field in 1993, they set the single-season major-league attendance record of 4,485,350.

The Astor House Museum portrays late 19th-century boarding house life.

of Littleton artifacts. Exhibits focus on such engaging themes as favorite toys through the decades.

Golden

"Welcome to Golden—Where the West Lives" proclaims an arch extending across the main street of Golden, a thriving community west of Denver. When the '59ers thronged to gold fields in nearby mountains, Golden City sprouted as a mining supply center. In 1862, the settlement was named the capital of the Colorado Territory. A major crossroads for both stagecoaches and freight wagons, the town initially prospered with the advent of the railroad. In the early 1870s, 23 trains passed daily through its rail switching facilities. That activity quickly subsided, however, when officials transferred the railroad headquarters from Golden to rival Denver.

Although the town lost its 19th-century leadership roles as territorial capital and railroad headquarters, it has held on tightly to its charm, historic riches and strong community spirit. A mural painted on the south wall of Foss Drug, for example, captures key figures, institutions and highlights of Golden's history. Among them is a depiction of the Colorado School of Mines, the nation's foremost school of mining

Rocky Mountain Brew

After stowing away on a ship bound for the United States and working his way west, in 1873 Adolph Coors succeeded in building his dream brewery in the foothills of Golden. The 25-year-old was no novice to brewing. Besides apprenticing for three years in his native Prussia, he worked as a brewery foreman in Illinois. By 1890, his company turned out nearly 18,000 barrels of beer per year. When Prohibition banned the manufacture and sale of alcoholic beverages, the entrepreneur implemented resourceful ways to keep afloat. The company began manufacturing porcelain and malted milk products as well as bottling a "cereal beverage," which contained less alcohol than the legal limit of 1/2 percent. The brewery's transition from heavy beer to a light variety in the 1960s created a stellar marketing hit. Soon "light" became an industry buzzword. Today, the family's fourth generation runs day-to-day operations. Producing more than 20 million barrels of beer per year, Coors Brewing Company is the world's largest single site brewery.

engineering. The ornate, multistory building that originally housed Coors Brewery rises on another section of the mural. Legendary showman William F. "Buffalo Bill" Cody, whom the town honors annually during Buffalo Bill Days, poses in western regalia. The mural also commemorates early landmarks that are now nonexistent: the town's first saloon; its first permanent structure; the Belle Vista Hotel; and the Tramway Depot.

Many of Golden's historic buildings, however, still stand. For example, three dozen landmark residences grace Twelfth Street Historic District. Their diverse architectural styles include Vernacular Masonry, Edwardian and whimsical Folk Victorian. Because many of the former residents were territorial representatives, the area was once called Legislative Walk. Other legislators boarded closer to Golden's main street in the Astor House Hotel, now a museum.

11. Astor House Museum
822 12th Street
(303) 278-3557
Open daily June through August, Tuesday through Saturday September through May
Admission charged
Located downtown at 12th and Arapahoe Streets

The stately stone structure's role as a residence for legislators evaporated when in 1867 Denver wrested the territorial capital title away from Golden. The hotel then evolved into a boarding house for miners, cowboys, families and travelers. The Astor House Museum depicts late 19th-century boarding house life with such furnishings as hand pump sinks and rope beds.

12. Golden Pioneer Museum
923 10th Street
(303) 278-7151
Open Monday through Saturday
Free
Located in downtown Golden

From an impressive Native American doll collection to the town's first galvanized bath tub, artifacts in the Golden Pioneer Museum relate how this community's early residents lived, primarily from 1859 to 1930. In addition, the museum houses the Mary Wallenhorst Johnson Research Center. Here, history buffs can investigate the lives of Golden pioneers by poring through an ex-

All Aboard!

Union Station greets rail travelers arriving at downtown Denver.

The impact of railroads on Colorado was practically immediate. Within two years of the trains' arrival, the populations of both Denver and the Colorado Territory doubled.

Compared to the horses, ox-drawn wagons and stagecoaches that transported people and goods across the plains until 1870, rail cars traveled rapidly and efficiently. Moreover, they eased relocation and expedited communication. The concepts of time and distance shrank. The Kansas Pacific stretched east from the capital while the Denver Pacific connected the city to the Union Pacific transcontinental railroad at Cheyenne, Wyoming Territory. Other railroads linked key Front Range locales. The Colorado Central, for example, laid a 15-mile track between Denver and Golden. The Denver & Rio Grande connected the capital to newly founded Colorado Springs. Additional lines spread within the territory to create better access to ore mines and coal fields. By 1890, the railroads had developed both sides of the Continental Divide and crossed all four of the state's borders.

tensive photograph collection, public records and numerous genealogical volumes.

13. Colorado Railroad Museum

17155 West 44th Avenue
(303) 279-4591, (800) 365-6263
Open year-round except Thanksgiving and Christmas
Admission charged
Twelve miles west of downtown Denver off Interstate 70 Exit 266; from Golden two miles east on 10th Street

At the foot of North Table Mountain, the Colorado Railroad Museum stokes rail buffs' fascination with acres of historic locomotives, cars and cabooses. A replica of an 1880s masonry depot exhibits memorabilia that illustrate the regional railroads' rich history. Among the items are train registers, headlights, maps, photos of wrecks, mud slides and rock slides, dining car menus and table settings, and inspection reports. On the lower level, miniature trains clickety-clack on an HO scale model railroad. On select weekends, plumes of smoke billow over Col-

orado's oldest operating steam locomotive—1881 narrow-gauge Denver & Rio Grande Western No. 346—as it transports passengers in cars and cabooses over the museum's half-mile line. Visitors may also ride in a 1930s vintage Galloping Goose rail car. The Robert W. Richardson Library makes available its thousands of books, photo collection and archives of railroad company documents for on-site research.

14. Clear Creek History Park

11th & Arapahoe Streets
(303) 278-3557
Open Wednesday through Sunday, mid-April through mid-October
Admission charged
Located on 11th Street between Cheyenne and Maple Streets

In historic Golden, Clear Creek History Park exhibits homestead cabins, farm buildings and a school relocated from Golden Gate Canyon. While miners swarmed to the gold fields around Black Hawk and Central City in the mid-1800s, homesteaders settled in the canyon, striking their own "riches" by supplying food to the burgeoning mining camps. Among the settlers was Thomas Pearce of Cornwall, England. The two cabins relocated to the history park are former residences of Pearce family members. Canyon homesteaders built Guy Hill School in 1876. Besides housing classrooms, the building served as a local gathering place, church, voting station and dance hall. A root cellar, meat house, and other period buildings further depict the homesteader lifestyle.

"Buffalo Bill" Cody's legendary life embodied the spirit of the West.

15. Buffalo Bill Memorial Museum and Grave

987 1/2 Lookout Mountain Rd.
(303) 526-0747
Open daily except Mondays
November through April and
Christmas Day
Admission charged
Thirty minutes west of downtown Denver off Interstate 70
Exit 236, or 6th Avenue West to
Golden, left onto Lariat Trail
(19th Street) and up to top of
mountain

Sitting atop Lookout Mountain, the Buffalo Bill Memorial
Museum and Grave honors
William F. Cody, the bison
hunter, scout and sharpshooter whose spectacular
Wild West Shows thrilled audiences throughout North
America and Europe. Elabo-

rate costumes, colorful posters
and other memorabilia trace
Cody's exciting life, including
his record-setting Pony Express ride at age 15. Exhausting a score of steeds, the
young horseman rode across
322 miles in only 21 hours and
40 minutes. He gained his
nickname "Buffalo Bill" while
working as a hunter for the
Kansas Pacific Railroad. In an
eight-month period, he
downed 4,200 bison to feed
the work crew. The museum
also features mementos of his
family and such fellow performers as Sitting Bull, Annie
Oakley and Lulu Parr. Galleries
exhibit paintings, sculptures
and other artwork depicting
Western scenes. Among them
are Frederick Remington's
"Portrait of a Ranch Hand"

and Robert O. Lindneux's
painting of Cody mounted on
his white stallion. Outside,
Cody's grave rests on the hilltop. When the celebrated
showman died in 1917, citizens of both Denver and Cody,
Wyoming—which he
founded—claimed the right to
inter him in their respective
towns. The Colorado capital
won out. Nevertheless, to deter any attempts to disturb
Buffalo Bill's gravesite on
Lookout Mountain, Denverites
entombed his remains under
several tons of steel reinforced
concrete.

Boulder

A group of gold-fevered 59ers
headed by Captain Thomas
Aikins chose to diverge from a
wagon train bound for Pikes

Shoppers stroll Boulder's pedestrian-only Pearl Street Mall lined with historic buildings.

Peak and head up the St. Vrain River to seek their fortune. Within a month after a prospector discovered a vein of gold, in 1859 Boulder City was founded. Soon the community boasted a schoolhouse, general store and post office. Some 70 log houses with pine splint roofs and dirt floors lined Pearl Street and the public square. Today the town honors its origins with Pearl Street Historic District, a local gathering place with trendy shops, night clubs and sidewalk cafes.

16. Pearl Street Historic District

Pearl Street
Open year-round
Free
Located between 11th and 15th Streets in downtown Boulder

Heavenly Sounds

Opera stars, rock vocalists and prominent world leaders have effortlessly projected their voices from the sandstone ledge that forms the stage of Red Rocks Amphitheater since its dedication in 1941. When George Ernest Cranmer became Denver's manager of improvements and parks, he spearheaded creation of this theater cradled in red sandstone formations. Construction began as soon as Cranmer obtained National Park Service approval, $300,000 of federal funds and permission to use Civilian Conservation Corps workers. Young CCC employees carved the rocks using picks, shovels and some explosives. A fleet of dump trucks, each capable of carrying only a modern pickup truckload, hauled away debris. When the outdoor theater officially opened, some 9,000 people sat between the two impressive crags forming its side walls, Creation Rock and Ship Rock. Metropolitan Opera soprano Helen Jepson flew from New York City to sing at the dedication. A 100-piece orchestra and 100-voice chorus accompanied her. After World War II, programs emphasized classical music, often performed by the Denver Symphony with guest artists such as Marian Anderson and Leonard Bernstein. Coloradans attended the amphitheater's first Easter sunrise service in 1947. Among the diverse celebrities who have attracted audiences since 1960 are Trini Lopez, the Kingston Trio, Ella Fitzgerald, Rod McKuen, Al di Miola, the Grateful Dead, and the Beatles.

Pearl Street Historic District Walking Map

1. Buckingham Block, 1101-1111 Pearl Street

Fanlights with grillwork, swags on the cornice and pilasters flanking second story windows distinguish this Federal-style building. Prior to its construction in 1898, a log cabin, later enlarged into a store, boarding house and residence, occupied the site.

2. Berlin-Boulder City Building, 1138 Pearl Street

Gold leaf ornamentation originally graced the facade to make it "the handsomest building in town." A massive, triangular pediment crowns the red brick structure, which has always housed retail businesses.

3. Brookfield-Holstein Building, 1245-47 Pearl Street

Extending a half-block, this is one of Boulder's oldest structures. A cornice with decorative relief and rounded bay window top its columned corner entrance.

4. Hotel Boulderado, 2115 13th Street

The sale of stock at $100 a share financed construction of this elegant hotel. A five-story cherry staircase and stained glass ceiling continue to grace the lobby. It has attracted such distinguished guests as Clarence Darrow, Robert Frost and Louis Armstrong.

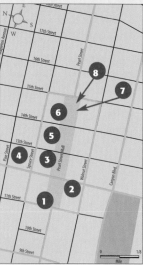

5. Boulder County Courthouse, 1325 Pearl Street

Built exclusively by unemployed Boulderites in the early 1930s, this striking structure exhibits the Art Deco/Art Moderne style. Distinctive features include a stepped silhouette and four-sided clock tower.

6. Boulder Theatre, 2032 14th Street

Theater architect Robert Boller designed this splendid Art Deco building. The stylized facade of stucco, terra cotta and glass sports brilliant colors. Restored original murals grace the interior.

7. Boulder Hardware Building, 1408-12 Pearl Street

This Italianate structure first housed a buggy business with lodging on the second floor. Typical of many commercial buildings in the late-19th century, it sports a mail-order, cast-iron storefront, complete with an embossed pediment and other intricate features.

8. Sternberg-Citizens National Bank Building, 1424-28 Pearl Street

Before its use as a bank, this structure served as a post office, creamery and even a dance hall. Egg-and-dart molding, fleur-de-lis and floral inset panels embellish the facade.

A group of education-minded citizens promised to ensure election of Charles L. Holly as Boulder Valley's territorial legislator in exchange for his pledge to pass a bill making the city the university site. Both succeeded. The city donated 52 acres of land to the institution and $15,000 to match the legislature's appropriation. The cornerstone of the university building was laid in September 1875.

Music in a Mountain Meadow

Located in Boulder, Chautauqua Park is a peaceful haven and cultural center.

Strains of classical music dance throughout Chautauqua's auditorium before squeezing between century-old wall boards into a poppy-filled meadow at the base of the Flatirons. Since Independence Day in 1898, this summer cultural mecca in Boulder has nurtured visitors with concerts, forums and such eclectic entertainment as silent movies with live piano accompaniment.

The concept of Chautauqua which began in the 1870s at Chautauqua Lake, New York, sought to immerse people in art, education, music and oratory. Thousands of Chautauquas soon sprang up around the country.

The Boulder location originated when a group of Texas teachers inquired about establishing a site in Colorado. Financed by a $20,000 bond issue, the city of Boulder and the University of Colorado bought the Batchelder orchard and built an auditorium and dining hall. The first attendees lodged in tents, but in subsequent years cottages created a permanent community. Today only three Chautauquas survive: New York's Chautauqua Lake, Ohio's Lakeside on Lake Erie and Boulder's Chautauqua.

Northern Front Range

Greeley celebrates Potato Day at Centennial Village Museum.

"**G**o West!" Horace Greeley's newspaper, the New York *Tribune*, encouraged readers as the country rebounded from the Civil War. Its columns spilled over with glowing accounts of Nathan Meeker's trip west and his vision of a utopian community at the base of the Rocky Mountains.

Hundreds embraced the dream. In the spring of 1870, the brave members of the Union Colony of Colorado settled on the parched high plains of northeastern Colorado Territory. The following year, the Chicago-Colorado Company established Longmont in the fertile St. Vrain Valley. And soon after, the Larimer County Land Improvement Company sold shares of stock that entitled purchasers to take up residence in a new town called Fort Collins. Despite grasshopper plagues and other devastating setbacks, the agricul-

tural settlements endured and thrive to this day.

Long before these colonies created permanent towns, Native Americans, explorers, traders and fur trappers traversed these high plains. Major Stephen Long, a U.S. Army topographical engineer, led an expedition along the Platte River through Nebraska and into Colorado. Long's Peak, which soars more than 14,000 feet high, bears his name.

Trapper's Trail stretched from Fort Laramie to Bent's Fort. Trading outposts with such names as Lupton, Jackson and St. Vrain sprouted

along the route. Fur trading flourished until silk hats replaced beaver toppers as the height of men's fashion.

17. Fort Vasquez Museum
13412 US Highway 85
Platteville
(970) 785-2832
Open daily Memorial Day to Labor Day, Wednesday to Saturday the rest of the year
Free
Less than one mile south of Platteville

Foremost among the trading posts on the South Platte River, Fort Vasquez operated

Left: Rugged mountains rise behind MacGregor Ranch Museum.

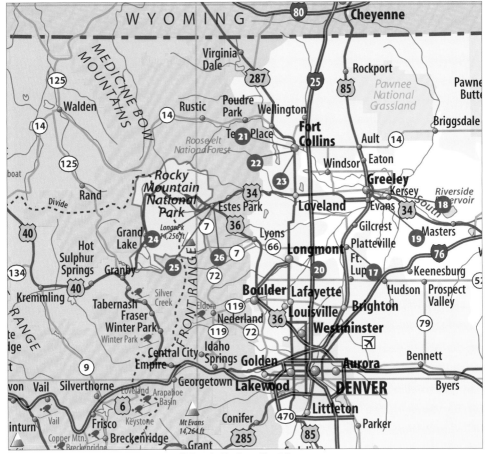

Colorado Northern Front Range

from 1835-1842. Inside its adobe walls, Cheyenne and Arapaho exchanged buffalo hides and beaver skins for awls, iron arrow heads and other prized items. Today, a reconstruction stands on the trading post site, wedged between US Highway 85's lanes. Inside the museum, displays and excavation findings interpret the fur trading era.

Greeley

A dozen miles north of the fort, the Union Colony of Colorado settled on land at the confluence of the South Platte

Nathan Meeker

Josephine Meeker's typewriter (1876).

Go West! When Nathan Meeker (1817-1879) visited the frontier to write accounts for Horace Greeley's New York *Tribune*, he became so enamored that he founded a utopian agricultural community, the Union Colony of Colorado. In 1870 colonists joined Meeker

Nathan Meeker

in establishing a farming settlement on the high plains. Although their town of Greeley prospered, Meeker wallowed in business debts. To earn money to pay them off, he became an Indian agent at White River Agency. Cultural clashes, such as Meeker's insistent demands that the hunter-oriented Utes become farmers, exploded into the White River Massacre, in which Meeker died.

and Cache la Poudre Rivers. To qualify for membership, colonists had to be literate, possess $1,000 in savings to see them through hard times and vow temperance. The $155 membership fee granted each family rail transportation west, including a full box car for furniture, and a chance to buy residential lots and farm land with access to irrigation and water rights. Thousands of trees shipped by rail beautified the new town, named after the West's fervent promoter, Horace Greeley.

In 1889, the state granted the town the first Normal School of Colorado, now the University of Northern Colorado. In later years, German-Russians and other ethnic groups migrated here to cultivate fields for the burgeoning sugar beet industry. Ranching and beef processing also became prominent, which the town annually honors with the Greeley Independence Stampede.

18. Meeker Home Museum
1324 Ninth Avenue
(970) 350-9220
Open mid-April through mid-October
Admission free
At 9th Avenue and 14th Street
south of Greeley Town Center

Spud Dudes

Greeley Independence Stampede is still going strong.

Since 1922, Greeley citizens have commemorated the Fourth of July with breath-arresting rodeo events. Befitting a region of potato fields, the first event was named the Spud Rodeo & Horseshow. Riding, roping, horseracing and pie eating contests highlighted the one-day, free celebration. To generate national recognition, in 1949 the organizers renamed the rodeo Go West With Greeley. Twenty-two years later they adopted its current title, the Greeley Independence Stampede, and added night shows headlining Johnny Paycheck, Loretta Lynn and other top entertainers. With stellar bronco riders, careening chuckwagons and mutton busting kids, the event has truly evolved into the World's Largest 4th of July Rodeo™.

Nathan Meeker built his two-story home one-half mile from the town center to give his colonists hope that Greeley would grow quickly. He chose adobe over scarce

Horace Greeley

and expensive lumber. The museum reveals family interests with such possessions as Meeker's cherry wood secretary, a clock with a lunar calendar for planting, and a copy of his wife's "spirit book," *Pilgrim's Progress*, on the bedroom dresser.

From Dust to Lush Fields

Early explorers decried the high plains as an uninhabitable wasteland, the Great American Desert. Founders of the early agricultural colonies, however, envisioned this region transformed by irrigation into abundant fields of sugar beets and golden wheat. Within two months of the arrival of the Union Colony of Colorado's first members, Ditch No. 3 coursed through Greeley, capable of irrigating 5,000 acres. The colony's first annual report exalts the irrigation system saying "the water came dancing through the flumes like a ministering angel, scattering blessings all along its path. It ran over the parched land, and blade and blossom awoke to a new beauty."

19. Centennial Village Museum

1745A St. at 14th Avenue
(970) 350-9220
Open mid-April through mid-October
Admission charged
Next to Grove Island Park

From a primitive shack to a picturesque Queen Anne style residence, Centennial Village chronicles the evolution of settlement in northeastern Colorado from 1860 to 1945. The unpretentious Carpenter House, an original Union

Colonist frame cottage, typifies Greeley's first homes. In this six-room residence, the Carpenters raised three sons, including a nationally recognized water law attorney. Several houses—a German-Russian shanty, an Hispanic adobe dwelling and a Swedish stuga—pay homage to the ethnic groups that settled here.

Longmont

Southwest of Greeley, the Chicago-Colorado Colony created the planned community of Longmont near the old

Colony Surveyor and Leader

Franklin C. Avery [1849-1923] played such an integral role in the development of Fort Collins that many of his contemporaries claimed his initials stood for Fort Collins. An original member of the Union Colony of Colorado, Avery came West to practice his trade as a surveyor and civil engineer. He platted Greeley's streets in 1871, then moved to Laporte where the Larimer County Land Improvement Company hired him to map out another town, Fort Collins. The young surveyor designed uncommonly wide streets lined with trees, many of which he himself transplanted from the foothills. While Avery surveyed most of the irrigation

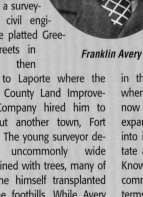

Franklin Avery

canals and roads serving the surrounding farms, he courted his upstate New York sweetheart by mail. Shortly after the couple married in 1876, Avery built a native red sandstone residence on Mountain Avenue. Numerous dormers and gables accented its roof line, creating an appearance that townspeople then described as "elaborate in style." Avery's leadership role in the community heightened when he established a bank, now the First National Bank, and expanded his business interests into irrigation, ranching, real estate and sugar beet processing. Known for his quiet dignity, the community leader served three terms as alderman.

Overland Stage route. Individuals of "strong moral character" could buy memberships for $155. The economy revolved around farming such crops as wheat, potatoes and sugar beets.

20. Longmont Museum
375 Kimbark Street
(303) 651-8374
Open year-round
Free
One block off Main Street between 3rd and 4th Avenues

The museum captures the lifestyle of early explorers and residents through interactive exhibits in the Long's Peak Room.

Fort Collins
To protect the region's stage lines, the military built a small post along the Cache la Poudre River, which the troops named after their commander, William O. Collins. When the army abandoned the post, the government opened the land to settlement. Larimer County Land Improvement Company acquired the property in 1872, platted a town named Fort Collins, and sold shares of stock that entitled the holders to lots. Howes, Medrum and many other original streets bear the names of company officials. For half a century, streetcars rolled down tree-lined avenues on the Fort Collins Municipal Railway. Today, restored Car 21 runs on summer weekends on the former Mountain Avenue line.

21. Old Town
College & Mountain Avenues
Open year-round
Free
Downtown triangle bounded by College Ave., Mountain Avenue and Jefferson Street.

Renovated in the 1980s, the former commercial district now sports trendy shops, restaurants and a sculpture studded plaza.

22. Fort Collins Museum
200 Matthews Street
(970) 221-6738
Open Tuesday through Sunday, closed Mondays and holidays
Free, donations welcome
Northeast of juncture of Mulberry Street and College Ave.

Exhibits emphasize the prominence of sugar beets and sheep in this region. In the courtyard, visitors can step inside a 19th century homesteader's cabin, a school house, and the town's first private dwelling, Elizabeth "Auntie" Stone's cabin. An astute businesswoman, Auntie converted her two-story residence into the area's first hotel.

23. Avery House
328 West Mountain Avenue
(970) 221-0533
Open Sundays and Wednesdays, except holidays
Free
At Meldrum Street, three blocks west of College Avenue

In the lovely home that surveyor Franklin Avery built in 1879, docents relate stories about the family through such heirlooms as a desk and ink well, chess set, and painting of

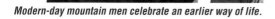

Modern-day mountain men celebrate an earlier way of life.

Fort Collins Old Town Walking Map

2. McHugh House and Hospital, 202 Remington
Because two of the owners of this impressive 1880s sandstone residence were mayors, locals call it the House of Mayors. Owner Peter J. McHugh, a doctor and mayor, converted the carriage house into a hospital.

3. Kissock Block, 117 E. Mountain
Decorative architectural details distinguish this brick structure.

1. Old Post Office, College & Oak
Italian Renaissance architectural elements grace the city's first post office building. It is now home to the Fort Collins Museum of Contemporary Art.

5. J.L. Honstein Block, 5 Old Town Square
Early businesses included a bakery, grocery and a chiropractic office, which advertised "No Surgery-No Medicine-No Faith-No Osteopathy." Coopersmith's Pub & Brewing now occupies the space.

4. Avery Block, 106 E. Mountain
Franklin Avery, the surveyor responsible for laying out the city's wide streets, established the First National Bank in this impressive sandstone structure. A lion's head guards the arched doorway.

6. Fire House, 232 Walnut
A distinctive bell tower crowns the structure that served as a fire station for nearly a century and as the first city hall.

7. Linden Hotel, 250 Walnut
Built in the 1880s to house the Poudre Valley Bank, this stately building became a hotel in 1917. A variety of businesses, including the post office, have occupied the ground floor.

Estes Park is the eastern gateway to Rocky Mountain National Park.

Mount Fuji. Made of local sandstone, the two-story residence underwent several additions, including the distinctive Queen Anne tower, complete with a custom-made curved radiator.

Estes Park

On a winter hunting expedition in 1860, Joel Estes happened upon a glorious glacial valley at the base of the Rocky Mountains and decided to settle there, making a livelihood by fishing, hunting and raising cattle.

With enactment of the Homestead Act, more pioneers settled in the valley. A crafty Irishman, Lord Dunraven, finagled 15,000 acres of land by hiring men to file dummy entries, then transferring the certificates to his company. For a time, much of the area became his private hunting preserve, accented by the magnificent English Hotel. Legitimate homesteaders eventually succeeded in exposing his land grab, causing Dunraven to sell most of his holdings and leave the valley.

At the turn of the 20th century, famed naturalist Enos Mills opened the Long's Peak Inn and inventor Francis O. Stanley built the stately Stanley Hotel. Vacationers generally stayed at least a month, scaling mountains, trekking on nature trails and relishing the pristine views.

Through the persistent efforts of Enos Mills and his supporters, Rocky Mountain National Park was dedicated in 1915. Trail Ridge Road, which traverses the Continental Divide, opened two decades later, making a vast portion of the natural preserve accessible to automobile travelers.

24. Estes Park Area Historical Museum
200 Fourth Street
(970) 586-6256
Admission charged
Open daily May through October, Friday to Sunday November through April
At US Highway 36 and Fourth Street

The main exhibit of the Estes Park Area Historical Museum spotlights the lives of early residents and visitors through photographs and distinctive artifacts, including a Stanley Steamer and wilderness etiquette instructions from naturalist Enos Mills' Long's Peak Inn. On the museum grounds, the Cobb-Macdonald Cabin shows the humble living quarters of early 20th-century residents. Standing nearby is the original National Park Service Headquarters. The white frame structure now houses special exhibits.

25. Enos Mills Cabin

6720 Highway 7
(970) 586-4706
Open Tuesday to Sunday in summer, Saturday and Sunday in winter
No admission charged; donations welcome
Eight miles south of Estes Park on Colorado Highway 7

A dirt path winds through ponderosa, lodgepole and limber pines to the one-room homestead cabin where Enos Mills, the founder of Rocky Mountain National Park, wrote many of his stories about nature and wildlife. Inside the sparsely furnished 1885 home, correspondence with Helen Keller and other mementos reveal the famous naturalist's spirited viewpoints.

26. MacGregor Ranch Museum

Devil's Gulch Road
(970) 586-3749
Open June, July and August
Donations welcome
Hwy. 34 bypass (Wonderview Avenue), right on MacGregor Avenue, right on Devil's Gulch Road

Nestled in a lush meadow, the MacGregor Ranch house opens onto glorious mountain views. Furnishings spanning three generations grace its rooms with Indian pottery, a chest of drawers designed to hold two huge lady's hats, a MacGregor clan blanket and other singular items. The six homestead papers hanging in the dining room reveal that the family homesteaded under three presidents: Grant, Hayes and Arthur. Besides raising Black Angus, the family ran a general store. A smoke house, root cellar and milk house border the residence.

Enos Mills: Father of Rocky Mountain National Park

Armed with an indomitable spirit, Enos Mills (1870-1922) tirelessly crusaded for the creation of Rocky Mountain National Park. As a 14-year old, he arrived in Colorado where he built a homestead cabin near Estes Park. The area's wondrous wildlife, flowers and geology captured his curiosity. When young Mills met John Muir, the famed naturalist encouraged him to record his observations. Mills developed his notes into 16 classic books, including *Wild Life on the Rockies* and *Grizzly: Our Greatest Wild Animal*. As owner of Long's Peak Inn, he shared his love of the land with guests through hikes, bird watching and climbs to the summit of towering, 14,255-foot Long's Peak. To pro-

Enos Mills and the Enos Mills Cabin.

tect the area's sublime natural environment, in 1909 Mills proposed establishment of a national park. Fulfillment of his vision required an intense personal lobbying effort fueled by dozens of public appearances and articles, and more than 2,000 hand-writ- ten letters. The U.S. Congress considered three different bills before passing legislation creating the preserve. Mills reaped the rewards of his perseverance when Rocky Mountain National Park was dedicated in 1915.

Right: The stately Stanley Hotel is an Estes Park landmark.
Inset: A Stanley Steamer is on display at the Stanley Hotel.

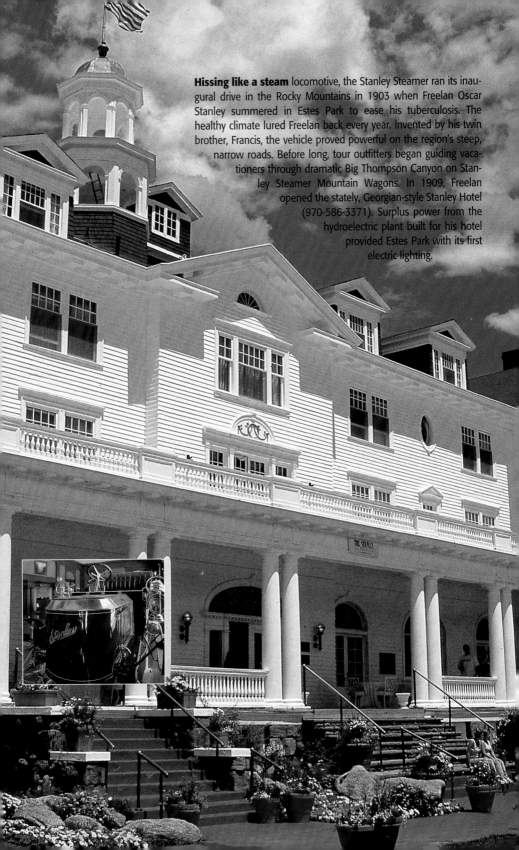

Hissing like a steam locomotive, the Stanley Steamer ran its inaugural drive in the Rocky Mountains in 1903 when Freelan Oscar Stanley summered in Estes Park to ease his tuberculosis. The healthy climate lured Freelan back every year. Invented by his twin brother, Francis, the vehicle proved powerful on the region's steep, narrow roads. Before long, tour outfitters began guiding vacationers through dramatic Big Thompson Canyon on Stanley Steamer Mountain Wagons. In 1909, Freelan opened the stately, Georgian-style Stanley Hotel (970-586-3371). Surplus power from the hydroelectric plant built for his hotel provided Estes Park with its first electric lighting.

Central Front Range

The Argo Gold Mill-Mine-Museum interprets the regions' mining era.

Determined to strike it rich, fortune seekers ventured beyond the Denver gold camps into the Rockies' rugged wilderness. At the confluences of Clear Creek and various mountain streams, early prospectors cried "Eureka!"

Within months, thousands of miners questing similar bonanzas poured into these sites, forming ramshackle settlements that evolved into today's Idaho Springs, Black Hawk, Central City, Georgetown and Silver Plume. Well-experienced in hard rock mining in their homelands, British, Cornish and Irish immigrants gravitated to the Clear Creek area. Mine tunnels soon perforated canyon walls. Because of its abundant supply of water, Black Hawk quickly became a key ore milling and smelting center. The economic boom created an environmental disaster: creeks polluted with sewage and industrial wastes, mountainsides stripped of timber cut for housing and mines, air contaminated with smelters' toxic fumes. At the same time, prosperity supported such refinements as the Central City Opera House. Moreover, the Colorado Central laid tracks as far as Silver Plume, transporting not only coal to fire mills, but also lush fabrics for draperies and such culinary delicacies as raw oysters. The bubble burst for the silver mines in 1893 when Congress repealed the Sherman Silver Purchase Act. By the turn of the 20th century, the cost of mining local precious metals outweighed their value on the market.

27. Hiwan Homestead Museum
4208 S. Timbervale Drive
(303) 674-6262
Open year-round Tuesday through Sunday
Free
Just off Meadow Drive near Highway 74, Evergreen

Left: Historic Georgetown nestles in Clear Creek Canyon in Colorado's Front Range.

This 17-room rustic mountain lodge showcases distinctive pioneer architecture in a serene mountain setting. A mixture of mountain mud, sand and honey chink the original portion's hand-adzed logs. When Mary Neosho Williams acquired the log structure in the 1880s, she hired a Scottish carpenter to convert it into a summer cottage. A signature feature is the main staircase, formed by setting quarter logs into a stringer carved from a single tree. Later, she added the octagonal two-story tower off the master bedroom. Many of the rooms represent the period of 1915 through 1930. Native American blankets and pottery reflect the avid interest of Williams' grandson, Frederic H. Douglas, in acquiring Indian handicrafts. His collection formed the nucleus of the Native American Arts collection at Chappell House, an early location of the Denver Art Museum. Later, an Oklahoma couple purchased the property naming it Hiwan Homestead, "a high secluded place with enough land for one ox to plow."

Colorado Central Front Range

Central City and Black Hawk

Hugging the slopes of Gregory Gulch, the historic mining-era towns of Central City and Black Hawk now strive to strike it rich through limited stakes gambling. Glittering casinos opened in October 1991, outshining the rock shops, bawdy bars and quaint structures that once attracted tourists. Some vestiges of the past, however, still sparkle like gems. The crown jewel is the Central City Opera House. During the gold mining boom, citizens raised funds to build a grand opera house befitting the town's reputation as "the richest square mile on earth." The 550-seat structure is now a National Historic Landmark. Each summer, it showcases such classics as Puccini's *La Boheme*. Other sites in Central City capture historic slices of life. The Thomas House Museum portrays the life style of a typical middle class family in the late 1800s. The Gilpin History Museum houses collections of kerosene lamps, vintage carriages and other local memorabilia. Call (303) 582-5283. Currently Black Hawk is assembling Mountain City Historic Park, comprised of 12 historically significant houses and structures. The park will eventually include the lovely Lace House. Decorative gable trim accents this Carpenter Gothic architectural treasure with delicate lacy detailing. Call (303) 582-5221.

Idaho Springs

Although George A. Jackson hoped to keep secret his 1859 discovery of placer gold, word spread quickly and droves of miners descended on Jackson's Diggings, now called Idaho Springs. Even now, mines extract riches from the area's mountainsides. One codger, Charlie Tayler, built a massive landmark for the community: a waterwheel at the base of Bridal Veil Falls, now viewable from Interstate 70. Each bucket on the 40-foot diameter structure can hold 15 gallons of water. Ironically, Tayler, attributed his robust health to never shaving or bathing.

28. Argo Gold Mill-Mine-Museum

2350 Riverside Drive
(303) 567-2421
Open April to September
Admission charged
Along Clear Creek in downtown Idaho Springs

Mine dumps frame the historic Argo Gold Mill on its mountainside setting. For 40 years, the facility processed diverse ores from mines that produced more than $100 million in precious metals. Near the mill, the Argo Tunnel extended four miles through the mountain to Central City, providing a conduit for transporting ore to the mill from numerous locations. Today, a half-scale replica of a narrow gauge train carries visitors to the Double Eagle Gold Mine, dug more than a century ago with pick and shovel, hand steel and sledge hammer, and then to the concentration mill. A self-guided tour brochure explains the stages of removing gold, silver and other precious metals from the host rock. Inside these quiet walls, the deafening sounds of machines crushing, grinding and pulverizing ore once reverberated. A museum displays hand tools of the early miners, various types of lighting lamps, equipment developed at the turn of the 20th century, and unique mineral specimens. In addition, an extensive collection of photographs depicts the work settings and lifestyles of the region's miners.

29. Phoenix Gold Mine

Trail Creek Road
(303) 567-0422
Open daily, year-round
Admission charged
West of town off Stanley Road
(I-70 frontage road)

Cornish, English and Welsh immigrants first worked the Phoenix Mine's rich veins of gold. Dating to 1872, the facility continues to extract ore to-

---

Central Front Range Recommendations

- **Experience the engineering** marvel of the Georgetown Loop Railroad on the scenic ride between Georgetown and Silver Plume.

- **Walk into the depths** of a mine shaft and learn the techniques of hardrock mining at the Phoenix Gold Mine or the Edgar Experimental Mine in Idaho Springs.

- **Stroll through Georgetown's** charming 19th-century commercial and residential streets.

- **In the Hamill House Museum** in Georgetown, view the luxurious possessions and decor that silver magnate William A. Hamill could afford to enjoy even in a remote mining community.

- **Admire the quality** craftsmanship and pioneer architecture of the Hiwan Homestead Museum.

Drill, Blast and Muck

Early hardrock miners typically endured 10-hour shifts in dark, damp shafts illumined only by candlelight. Striking sledge hammers against steel bars, they hand drilled blast holes at a rate of about three feet an hour. When enough holes perforated the wall, the "blasting monkey" loaded them with flash powder and lit the detonating cord. Mucking, or shoveling the crumbled ore into mine cars, followed. For their labor, 1870s miners earned up to $3.50 a day. Eager to increase their take, many "high-graded" gold and silver by stashing crumbled metal in cigarette butts or rubbing flecks in their hair. Equipment improvements, such as drills powered by compressed air, speeded the drilling process. Unfortunately, early models generated high levels of dust that caused a deadly lung disease, silicosis, earning them the nickname "widow makers." By the turn of the 20th century, drills using water to minimize dust replaced their lethal predecessors.

Georgetown Walking Map

**4. Kneisel-Curtis-Seifried Building,
6th between Rose and Taos Streets**
Four generations of the Kneisel-Anderson family served the community with a grocery and hardware business.

**1. Bowman-White House,
906 Rose Street**
With a silver mine supervisor and an attorney as its first owners, this Queen Anne two-story house reflects the lifestyle of Georgetown's early managerial and professional groups. Behind the residence, Historic Georgetown, Inc. also conserves a log cabin and a typical 1870s miner's home.

**3. Hotel de Paris,
6th near Taos Street**
Statuary crowned Louis Dupuy's fine hotel. A single masonry facade covers three buildings joined together for lodging, a restaurant and his living quarters.

**5. Masonic Hall,
6th near Rose Street**
A decorative cornice tops this brick Italianate structure. The upstairs continues to house the Masonic Lodge. Retailers occupy the street level.

**2. Star Hook and Ladder Firehouse,
6th near Griffin Street**
This early volunteer fire company tackled fires with such advanced equipment as long trucks with ladders, hook stakes and leather buckets. The building now serves as the town hall.

**8. Hamill House,
305 Argentine Street**
A statue tops the fernery plant stand that fills the center of the Hamill House's inviting glass solarium. The floorboards are spaced so that air from the basement can rise between them.

6. Fish Block, 6th at Rose Street
After fire destroyed the wood structure, Charles R. Fish rebuilt the Bank of Clear Creek County in brick. Retail businesses now occupy the building.

**7. Alpine Hose No. 2,
5th Street near Taos Street**
Mining magnate William A. Hamill bought the bell for this fire station's 65-foot tower.

Impressive facades line Georgetown's Sixth Street.

day. During tours, present-day miners describe area history, mining processes and "tommyknockers," the imaginary elf-like creatures that Cornish miners blamed for mysterious occurrences and mischief deep inside the shafts. Visitors can labor for their own sparkling nuggets by drilling in the manner used in the 1860s: hand steeling. After hammering a steel bar onto a gold-bearing vein and then turning the implement with a "hit, quarter-turn, hit quarter-turn" rhythm, wannabe miners soon find their efforts rewarded.

30. Edgar Experimental Mine

365 Eighth Avenue
(303) 567-2911
Open Memorial Day to Labor Day
Admission charged
At Colorado Blvd.

This working mine also serves as an underground laboratory

for Colorado School of Mines students. The Miami Tunnel, in which students and staff lead one-hour public tours, lies 500 feet below the mountain top and penetrates 2,000 feet. Because this site also conducts equipment testing, mine rescue training programs, and mining operations and safety courses, its tours enthrall hard rock mining enthusiasts with detailed technical focus. Guides describe and demonstrate the various drills used historically to prep walls for blasting. Nearby lie examples of a detonating cord, safety fuse, shock tubes and other critical items. A muck shovel and ore car represent the final stage of the drill, blast, muck operation. To emphasize what miners encounter when the electricity trips off, the guide turns off the lights. Not even a hand held right in front of one's eyes is discernible.

Georgetown and Silver Plume

A few miles upstream from the mining frenzy around Idaho Springs and Central City, two brothers from Kentucky, George and David Griffith, discovered gold flecks while panning at the confluence of Clear Creek and South Clear Creek. Their humble mining camp became known as Georgetown. Although gold attracted the first wave of prospectors, the discovery of silver created a boom that lasted more than two decades. By 1870, some 3,000 souls resided in this commercial center. Numerous mills crushed ore. Stately churches, a school and flagstone sidewalks reflected the town's burgeoning affluence. Solid brick buildings, now filled with restaurants, boutiques and galleries, lined the business district on Sixth

Street. Elegant houses showcased such notable architectural styles as Gothic Revival, Italianate and Queen Anne. In them, bank presidents, ore processing speculators, silver barons and other powerful citizens resided. More than 200 of the community's original buildings still stand.

While mostly managerial and professional people resided in Georgetown, mining families gravitated to neighboring Silver Plume, two miles up Clear Creek Canyon. Some say Silver Plume's name was inspired by a vein of silver so rich that silver flakes broke off in featherlike patterns. A disastrous fire leveled the town's core of wood frame buildings in 1884. Historic structures viewable today include several post-fire stores on Main Street, the massive Romanesque building that once housed the school and the Silver Plume Bandstand, where the Terrible Mine band and other musical groups performed. In 1877, the Colorado Central Railroad reached Georgetown, linking the mining region to Denver and the East. Several years later the ambitious engineering feat of extending the line up the formidable grade to Silver Plume was completed. The two towns enjoyed prosperity until Congress repealed the Sherman Silver Purchase Act in 1893, thus placing the country on a gold standard. Silver mining fortunes vanished overnight. As residents sought employment elsewhere, the communities fell into neglect and ruin. The area began to revive in 1966 when the valley was designated the Georgetown-Silver Plume National

Historic Landmark. Today, Georgetown's 19th-century commercial and residential structures represent the lifestyle of the mining boom's movers and shakers. Inside the facility that has produced electricity continuously since 1900, the Georgetown Energy Museum (303) 569-3557 relates the importance of hydroelectric power to the second stage of mining. Neighboring Silver Plume's modest dwellings and stores illustrate the setting in which mining families lived. Connecting the two communities, the Georgetown Loop Historic Mining and Railroad Park reveals both the daily labors of hard rock miners and the railroad's vital role.

31. Hamill House Museum

305 Argentine Street
(303) 569-2840
Open daily Memorial Day through September; Sat-Sun through mid-December
Admission charged

Three blocks off Sixth Street The features of this Country Style Gothic Revival house boast silver magnate William A. Hamill's successes in mining speculation, transportation, ranching and communications. Elegant drapes "puddle" onto the parlor floor, delicate English tiles frame the fireplaces and tiers of greenery thrive in the sun-drenched conservatory. Embossed wallpaper resembling hand-tooled leather covers the library walls. Black walnut woodwork trims doorways and windows.

L.C. Boyington Salesmen's Desk-Beds

By day a desk.

By night a bed.

Rail access to Georgetown

in the late 1870s spurred increasing numbers of traveling businessmen to visit the remote mountain town. Keen to accommodate this growing clientele, Hotel de Paris owner Louis Dupuy designed two rooms to address their commercial needs. During business hours, the merchants greeted customers in the large, high-ceilinged "sample rooms," displaying their wares and writing orders at impressive, wood desks. Chandeliers with cobalt blue gaslight shades brightened the area while centralized steam heat warmed the transactions. After hours, the rooms transformed into typical accommodations when the desks unfolded into beds, complete with horsehair mattresses.

Crowned with a cupola, even the family privy exhibits a distinctive style. At the rear of the property the entrepreneur built stately granite structures for his carriage house, stable and business offices.

32. Hotel de Paris Museum

409 Sixth Street
(303) 569-2311
Open daily Memorial Day through September;

Skinny Rails

Chugging up Clear Creek Canyon.

While the standard gauge for railroad tracks measured 56 1/2" wide, the Colorado Central Railroad laid tracks only 36 inches apart for its route to Georgetown. The three-foot spacing made it possible for trains to turn tighter curves and climb steeper grades.

As it wound up Clear Creek to Central City and over extraordinary Georgetown Loop into the mining community of Silver Plume, the narrow gauge railroad slipped locomotives and ore cars through tight canyons, over turbulent streams, and alongside sheer mountain passes. Such lines were common in the Colorado mountains from 1871 until the late 1940s.

Sat-Sun through December
Admission charged
Between Taos and Griffith Streets

After a checkered past as a seminarian, news reporter and army deserter, Frenchman Louis Dupuy transformed a Georgetown bakery into an upscale hotel that boasted the most modern amenities of the 1880s, including gravity-fed hot and cold running water in each guest room. As a conservation feature, he installed sinks with "rabbit ear" faucets that released water only while users held them open. Silver maple and black walnut floors line the elegant dining room, while frescoes grace the walls and Limoges Haviland china glistens on the tables. A private library of 2,600 volumes attests to Dupuy's scholarly bent.

33. Georgetown Loop Railroad

1106 Rose Street
(303) 569-1000
Open Labor Day Weekend to early October
Admission charged; purchase tickets at the Old Georgetown Depot, 11th and Argentine Streets
Depots at end of Loop Drive off Argentine Street in Georgetown and at Silver Plume Interstate 70 Exit 226

The extraordinary engineering feat known as the Georgetown Loop, which more than a century ago made it possible for locomotives to climb the steep elevation from Georgetown to neighboring Silver Plume, continues to marvel today's travelers. Aboard open-air rail coaches pulled by a coal-pow-

---

ered steam locomotive, passengers ride across Devil's Gate High Bridge some 100 feet above Clear Creek. The track crosses over itself, passes the Lebanon Mine and Mill Complex, and then continues to scale the slope through other twists and turns before it reaches the Silver Plume depot.

Although tourists became the railroad's primary customers shortly after the "loop" was completed in 1884, the Colorado Central Railroad undertook this challenging endeavor with only one motive—extend the line to the wealth-bearing silver mines of Leadville. Only two miles separated Georgetown and Silver Plume, but in that short distance the elevation gained 638 feet, greater than a six percent grade. Since locomotives could negotiate a four percent grade at most, engineers had to design a means to lay 4 1/2 miles of track in two miles. The remarkable loop design resulted. The incentive to continue building this railroad westward died when a competing company laid tracks to Leadville. The line between the two mountain towns then evolved into a tourist attraction.

Today, passengers enjoy a round-trip ride past slopes laced with aspens and views of Republic Mountain's towering barren slopes, which bore such riches as the Hise Lode's four-inch wide veins of silver. Those departing from the Silver Plume depot can extend the trip with a tour of the Lebanon Mine and Mill Complex.

Southern Front Range

The Sangre de Cristo Mountains etch the horizon west of legendary Cripple Creek.

W hen Lt. Zebulon Pike explored the area in 1806, he disparaged the sagebrush prairie as a wasteland unsuitable for settlement. For the next 50 years, his assessment discouraged all but trappers, traders and a few courageous pioneers from adventuring into the area.

William Becknell's lucrative trade expedition to Santa Fe in 1821 launched international commerce on the Santa Fe Trail. Merchants plying the Mountain Route re-supplied at Bent's Fort on the Arkansas River. Strategically located on the trail near the base of Raton Pass, the predominantly Hispanic ranching community of Trinidad prospered. Under the Treaty of Guadalupe Hidalgo, which ended the Mexican War, the United States acquired substantial territory, including what now comprises Colorado's southeastern segment. Discovery of gold near

present-day Denver set off a stampede of '59ers bellowing "Pikes Peak or Bust." Pueblo, Cañon City and other supply towns sprouted like desert flowers after a rainstorm. Colorado City grew as a way station for prospectors before they scaled the Ute Trail to mountain mines. For a few days, Colorado City served as the territorial capital, but finding its dining and lodging facilities lacking, the legislators moved the capital to Golden. The construction of the Denver and Rio Grande Railroad advanced development southward. Railroad magnate Gen-

eral William Jackson Palmer founded Colorado Springs in 1871 as a model community and co-founded Manitou Springs as a health resort near effervescent waters that Utes believed sacred. As promotion of the region's therapeutic climate traveled East, health-seekers, especially those with respiratory ailments, gravitated to the towns. In 1872, Palmer extended the railroad to Pueblo, where he established the Colorado Fuel and Iron Company. Area coal mines fueled the thriving iron and steel mill. The proximity of railroad shipping points

Left: Pikes Peak rises skyward beyond Rock Ledge Ranch Historic Site at the Garden of the Gods.

Colorado's First US Explorer

Shortly after the Louisiana Purchase, Lieutenant Zebulon Montgomery Pike (1779-1813) and a party of some 75 men set out to explore and map the southwestern portion of the vast acquisition. Following the Arkansas River west, they searched for the Red River,

Zebulon M. Pike

then considered the boundary between the Louisiana Territory and Mexico.

In 1806, the Lieutenant sighted a mammoth mountain rising from the plains. With inadequate provisions and equipment, Pike's party attempted to reach its 14,110-foot summit only to be repelled by a November blizzard. Proclaiming that no man would ever ascend the landmark, Pike named it Grand Peak. In 1820, however, Dr. Edwin James, a scientist and historian on Major Stephen H. Long's expedition, succeeded in climbing to the top. The mountain was renamed Pikes Peak in honor of the earlier explorer's discovery.

Zebulon Pike rose to the rank of general before his death in the War of 1812. His exploration of the Louisiana Territory produced the first detailed report and maps of present-day eastern Colorado.

Colorado Southern Front Range

also stimulated Trinidad's cattle industry. The region's prosperity surged with the discovery of gold in 1890 in Poverty Gulch southwest of Pikes Peak. Colorado's richest gold camp, Cripple Creek, extracted well over half a billion dollars worth of gold. Meanwhile, the area continued to attract vacationers. After an excursion up Pikes Peak, Katharine Lee Bates celebrated Colorado's grandeur with her composition, "America the Beautiful."

Southern Front Range Recommendations

• **Visit the medical heritage** gallery in the Colorado Springs Pioneers Museum to learn how sanitoriums helped tuberculosis sufferers recover.

• **Sample the mineral waters** of Manitou Springs during a complimentary "Springabout" walking tour of the charming historic district.

• **Feast your eyes** on lustrous wood paneling, glimmering chandeliers and lush furnishings while exploring Pueblo's Rosemount Mansion and its 37 rooms.

• **Tour the Cripple Creek District Museum** to relive life in the boom times, then walk among the mine ruins in Vindicator Valley.

• **Discover how Trinidad** lifestyles evolved from the Santa Fe Trail era to arrival of the railroad at the Trinidad History Museum.

Colorado Springs

Envisioning a community for refined society, railroad magnate General William Jackson Palmer created a subsidiary of his Denver and Rio Grande Railroad to establish Fountain Colony at Pikes Peak. Teetotalers of good moral character could obtain membership by purchasing a $100 land certificate and a lot. In 1871, Palmer founded and named his town Colorado Springs, even though the closest springs bubbled four miles away. Within 18 months of groundbreaking, the population reached 1,500. Wide streets, parks, and high quality shops and restaurants enhanced its appeal. With one in five of its residents British-born, the town became known as "Little London." The establishment of Colorado College, the Colorado Springs Opera House and St. Francis hospital attested to the steadily growing city's stability. Besides vacationers, the climate's therapeutic qualities drew people suffering from respiratory ailments, especially tuberculosis. A thriving health industry

evolved. When gold was discovered in Cripple Creek in 1891, throngs of prospectors rushed to the area. Countless newcomers and residents such as Winfield Scott Stratton struck it rich, pouring their wealth back into Colorado Springs. By the turn of the 20th century, the population topped 30,000. Pikes Peak attractions, which millionaire entrepreneur Spenser Penrose skillfully promoted through the 1930s, continue to foster tourism.

34. Colorado Springs Pioneers Museum
215 South Tejon Street
(719) 385-5990
Open Tuesday to Sunday, May through October; Tuesday through Saturday, November through April
Free
Between Cucharras and Vermijo Avenues

Housed in the stately, former El Paso County Courthouse, the museum collection emphasizes cultural and historic elements unique to the Pikes

General Palmer's Colorado Springs

General William Jackson Palmer's [1836-1909] vision of a north-south railroad from Colorado to Mexico was too radical for his employer, the Kansas-Pacific, so in 1871 the Civil War veteran launched his own railroad, the Denver and Rio Grande. Concurrently, he established a subsidiary, the Colorado Springs Company, to

William Jackson Palmer

found a fashionable summer retreat for socialites near the base of Pikes Peak. Shortly thereafter, Palmer's locomotives steamed south to the Arkansas River, where another subsidiary established South Pueblo, and eventually into Cañon City. In Pueblo, steel soon rolled out of another of the railroad magnate's companies, Colorado Fuel and Iron.

Peak region. Among them are exhibits of Van Briggle art pottery, paintings of local scenes, and regional Indian artifacts. The medical heritage gallery chronicles Colorado Springs' role as a health resort, especially as the mecca for tuberculosis sufferers from 1890 to 1920. An original six-sided tuberculosis tent shows sanitorium patients' typical quarters.

35. McAllister House Museum

423 North Cascade Ave.
(719) 635-7925
Open Wednesday to Sunday, May through August; Thursday to Saturday, September through April
Admission charged
Between St. Vrain and Boulder Streets

To symbolize his belief in the permanence of his new community, the director of the Colorado Springs Company, Major Henry McAllister, built a sturdy brick house with iron rods anchoring its roof to withstand even the wildest chinooks. The elegant parlor features the gentleman's chair, lady's chair and ottoman that the family brought by train. The major's library holds several other original pieces, including his Civil War canteen and sword. In the dining room, such items as a teaspoon warmer, egg boiler and hot chocolate pot emphasize the British influence on the lifestyle of "Little London," as Colorado Springs was called.

36. Western Museum of Mining & Industry

1025 North Gate Road
(719) 488-0880
Open daily June through September, Monday through Saturday rest of year
Admission charged
East on I-25 Exit 156A
Gleneagle Drive

Multi-ton steam engines, drills and other restored equipment, operated by staff during daily guided tours, highlight the museum's collection. Many items originally served Colorado's richest gold camp, Cripple Creek. An enlightening display shows minerals and common household products that contain them. The interactive venue includes gold panning, single jacking and

Master Promoter

A formal fountain graces the entrance to The Broadmoor

When Philadelphia entrepreneur Spencer Penrose (1865-1939) opened The Broadmoor in 1918, guests experienced a quality of service unparalleled in the West. The resort's Italian Renaissance style exuded grandeur and wealth with such distinctive features as a curved marble staircase and pink stucco facade. An 18-hole golf course rolled across the expansive grounds. A master promoter, Penrose transformed the resort into a major destination by enhancing the touristic value of the region. First he built the Pikes Peak Road leading to the summit and initiated an annual auto race named the Pikes Peak Hill Climb. He established the Cheyenne Mountain Zoo. And in 1925, he purchased and modernized the Pikes Peak Cog Railway.

Along with expanding its facilities and amenities, The Broadmoor (800-634-7711) has maintained the historic richness of the original structure for the enjoyment of today's guests.

Costumed interpreters demonstrate old-time cooking skills at Rock Ledge Ranch Historic Site

weighing oneself in troy ounces.

37. Rock Ledge Ranch Historic Site
1401 Recreation Way
(719) 578-6777
Open Wednesday to Sunday, June to Labor Day; Saturday and Sunday in September. Admission charged

Off 30th Street across from Garden of the Gods Visitor Center

With dramatic Garden of the Gods as its backdrop, this site interprets Native American life from 1755 to 1835 as well as the evolution of lifestyles in Camp Creek Valley from 1867 to 1910. Outside a humble homestead cabin, costumed interpreters split wood and cook turnip stew. Walter Galloway worked this land under the Homestead Act of 1862 until Robert Chambers bought him out to establish Rock Ledge Ranch. The newcomer pioneered successful agricultural practices. By diverting water from the creek through irrigation ditches and into a small reservoir, he turned the arid soil into fruitful farmland. Today, interpreters bedecked in period clothing tend fields that demonstrate his irrigation method. His family resided in Rock Ledge House. Chambers later sold his land to General William Jackson Palmer. In 1907, relatives of the general moved into the country estate's newly built Orchard House. The home boasted steam heating, electric lighting and Arts and Crafts-style furnishings, all befitting the social stature of its residents.

Old Colorado City

Strategically located at the east entrance of Ute Pass, El Dorado, incorporated by Colorado City in 1859, served as a supply center for gold miners heading west. Ranchers, farmers, freighters and outfitters populated the one-time territorial capital. After Cripple Creek struck gold in 1891, the town boasted a railroad terminal and four gold ore reduction mills. With prosperity came the notoriety of its Red Light Row and 21 rowdy saloons on Colorado Avenue between 24th and 28th Streets. Today, boutiques and galleries line the avenue. In 1917, Colorado Springs annexed the community, now known as Old Colorado City.

Health Mecca of the West

Consumption, later called tuberculosis, racked 19th-century America. Early accounts by trappers and explorers proclaimed the healing powers of the West's alpine fresh air, sunshine and mineral spring waters. Aided by physicians' reports of miracle cures, Colorado Springs launched a nationwide campaign promoting the community as a glorious health resort. Wealthy consumptives lodged in elegant hotels and private residences. As word spread, "lungers" of lesser means and their families flocked to the city. By the 1880s, Colorado Springs suffered such a severe housing shortage that tent encampments sprouted like weeds in town parks, along riverbeds and on hillsides. Fear of contamination caused physicians to promote establishment of countryside sanitoriums. In response, fraternal, religious and labor organizations built institutions to treat tuberculosis. Cragmor and other luxurious, private facilities catered to the well-to-do. The daily sanitorium regimen of three full meals, exercise, sunshine and sleeping in the open air helped many patients regain their health.

Manitou Springs Walking Tour

**1. Briarhurst Manor,
404 Manitou Avenue**
Town founder Dr. William Bell built this pink sandstone Tudor manor in 1876 as his residence. It now houses an award-winning restaurant.

2. Barker House, 819 Manitou Ave.
Several grand hotels accommodated visitors during the town's health resort era. The building now contains a restaurant and senior residence.

**3. Wheeler Town Clock,
Manitou and Cañon Avenues**
Hygeia, the Greek goddess of health, stands atop the clock that Jerome Wheeler, a president of Macy's department store, presented to the city. Wheeler brought his wife here in the 1880s for her health.

4. Commonwheel Artists Cooperative, 102 Cañon Avenue
Located in the historic district, this co-op has provided for more than a quarter century a venue for local artists and craftspeople to display and sell their original work. Since its founding, the town has attracted artists to its glorious setting.

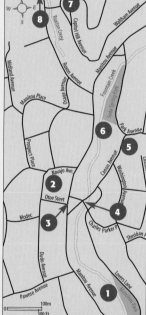

**5. The Cliff House @ Pikes Peak,
306 Cañon Avenue (888) 212-7000**
Restored to the Victorian elegance that attracted wealthy guests in the early 1900s, the inn recently re-opened with 57 lovely guest suites, fine dining and 21st-century amenities.

6. Historic Manitou Spa Building, between Manitou and Park Avenues
Travelers and residents once gathered in the Spa Building's open pavilion to savor Soda Spring's bubbly water. Neglected for many years, the structure currently is undergoing renovation.

7. Miramont Castle, 9 Capitol Hill
Nine styles of architecture as diverse as English Tudor and Byzantine distinguish this unique historic residence constructed of locally quarried greenstone, now a museum.

**8. Pikes Peak Cog Railway,
515 Ruxton Avenue**
In 1891, the first passenger train scaled to the 14,110-foot summit of Pikes Peak. Zalmon Simmons, inventor and founder of the Simmons Beautyrest Mattress Company, financed construction of the railway.

Major McAllister's desk in the McAllister House Museum.

38. Old Colorado City History Center

1 South 24th Street, Colorado Springs
(719) 636-1225
Open Tuesday through Sunday
Free
South 24th St. and Pikes Peak Avenue

Housed in a stately former church, the museum relates the town's historic role through artifacts and mural-size photographs, including one that shows miners trudging up Pike's Peak to the gold fields. Wooden beer mugs and decks of cards highlight an exhibit about Colorado Avenue's infamous saloons and broth-

els. In another display, native silver, pyrite and other area minerals gleam.

Manitou Springs

The medicinal properties of cool mineral waters rising naturally from limestone aquifers attracted Indians, trappers and traders to the box canyon in which Manitou Springs rests long before Dr. William Bell, an English adventurer, and General Palmer co-founded the town in 1872. Ute, Arapaho and other Indian tribes considered the mineral springs sacred. As the legend goes, the god Manitou breathed into the waters infusing them with effervescence and medicinal powers. Before settlement, explorers and prospectors lauded their benefits. Bell sought to transform the spring-fed canyon into a world-class health resort. By the late 1890s, "Saratoga of the West" bubbled with success. A magnificent bath house and seven elegant hotels, including the recently renovated Cliff House @ Pikes Peak, pampered health seekers, especially tuberculosis sufferers. Original Manitou Sparkling Water rolled off bottling lines for shipment to distant cities. Excursions up Pikes Peak further enhanced the resort's allure. The town's economy, however, collapsed in the 1960s when Highway 24 bypassed the community. The mineral springs that had brought such bounty became viewed as nuisances. Fortunately, formation of a national historic district in the 1980s regenerated enthusiasm in the town's rich history. Restoration recaptured its charming

Bubbling Waters

In Manitou Springs, a "sip of the bubbly" means a swig of water with an attitude. Strolling the historic district, one can sample cool liquids gurgling up from area mineral springs into public drinking fonts. Each spring sports a distinct flavor. The waters of Iron Spring Geyser, for example, taste like a daily mineral supplement. Locals favor cold, sweet and highly carbonated Twin Springs, especially for lemonade. Stratton Spring startles sippers when it sporadically erupts like a mini-geyser. Throughout the summer, the town sponsors "Springabouts," free guided tours highlighting its rich history, architecture and springs. For full enjoyment, take along a cup.

Cripple Creek Walking Tour

1. Cripple Creek & Victor NGRR, Bennett at 5th

Today, a four-mile round-trip track transports visitors along the former Colorado-Midland Line railway, which once carried trainloads of gold and supplies.

4. Cripple Creek City Hall, 337-343 E. Bennett Avenue

This stately two-story structure housed the board of aldermen, clerk's and treasurer's offices and the central fire department. Unlike in most communities of the time, its firemen were paid, not voluntary.

2. Gold Mining Stock Exchange, 373-379 E. Bennett Avenue

The stock exchange association that occupied this building sold an estimated $34 million of Cripple Creek mine shares in 1899 alone. The rusticated sandstone and corbelled brick building was one of the largest structures built after the city's devastating 1896 fires.

5. Becker & Nolon Block, 301 E. Bennett Avenue

Owners and financiers of several mining companies, Becker and Nolon ran a posh saloon in this ornately decorated building. They also operated a liquor company and investment firm here.

3. J. S. Neall Block, 361-363 E. Bennett Avenue

Designed specifically for Neall's assaying work, the building housed an assay office in the front and a sampling works in the back. Offices filled the upper stories.

6. Turf Club, 237-239 E. Bennett Avenue

This attractive Italianate building housed exclusive gentlemen club rooms for the city's most successful businessmen. Off-white, Norman brick graced the lower part of the facade, contrasting with the standard burnt orange brick used throughout the business district.

Remnants of the Vindicator Mine tower over Vindicator Valley.

40. Pikes Peak Cog Railway

515 Ruxton Avenue
(719) 685-5401
Open late April through late October
Admission charged
End of Ruxton Avenue

The world's highest cog railway winds 9 miles up Pikes Peak at a 25 percent grade. Cherry-red, Swiss-made rail cars transport passengers past tumbling streams, colossal boulders and fragrant Ponderosa pine forests to the vast, rocky terrain above timberline. While yellow-bellied marmots sunbathe atop granite ledges, Rocky Mountain bighorn sheep scale the slopes. At the 14,110-foot summit, expansive vistas of the Great Plains and rugged Sangre de Cristo Mountains unfold. Passengers have adequate time to enjoy the lofty view and purchase mementos before boarding for the beautiful descent.

Cripple Creek

Colorado's final mining bonanza blasted into a $600 million fortune after Bob Womack struck a small find of gold ore in the winter of 1890 in an area he had ironically named Poverty Gulch. Measuring four by six miles, Cripple Creek Mining District formed that spring. A few months later, Winfield Scott Stratton's claim yielded millions of dollars of gold. The rush to riches spiraled. Soon, nearly 500 mines tapped the ancient volcano's veins, and dozens of thriving towns dotted the hillsides. Three railroads transported riches to distant mills. By the turn of the 20th century, some 50,000 people called Cripple

character. Nine of the mineral springs are again accessible to the public. With this rebirth, an art colony has grown and prospered. And, bringing Manitou Springs full circle, a healing arts community again is flourishing.

39. Miramont Castle Museum

9 Capitol Hill Avenue
(719) 685-1011, (888) 685-1011
Open daily in summer, reduced hours and closed Mondays rest of year.
Admission charged
Off Ruxton Avenue

An eclectic architectural style, whimsical room shapes and extraordinary features characterize the 46-room mansion that a French Catholic priest built in 1895 for his widowed mother. Sunlight streams through Romanesque, Gothic and Moorish windows, just a sampling of the castle's nine types of architecture. Rooms with only four walls are rare: the conservatory has six; the chapel, eight; the guest bedroom, 16. The drawing room sports an imposing hand-cut stone fireplace weighing some 400,000 pounds.

Creek home. Vestiges of that era still cling to the slopes. Two-mile, interpretive Vindicator Valley Trail winds among ruins of the boom days, including Vindicator Mine's boardinghouses, powder igloos, blacksmith shop and rusted sheet metal building that marks the mine entrance. Today, extraction continues as the Cripple Creek & Victor Gold Mining Company surface mines 225,000 ounces of gold annually at the Cresson site. In addition, the Globe Reclamation Pad processes gold from old mine dumps through a leaching process, then reclaims the land by neutralizing the soil and planting aspens.

41. Mollie Kathleen Gold Mine
Highway 67
(719) 689-2466
Open 9 a.m. to 5 p.m. daily, April through October; off-season weekends, weather permitting
Admission charged
One mile northeast of town on Highway 67

After fortuitously spotting wire gold on a hike in 1891, Mollie Kathleen Gortner rushed to register a claim. The resultant mine operated for some 70 years. Today, visitors can squeeze into a nine-man cage and ride 1,000 feet down into the mine's dark depths. Former miners who worked gold veins for decades conduct the informative tour.

42. Cripple Creek District Museum
5th and Bennett Streets
(719) 689-2634
Open daily Memorial Day through September, weekends the rest of the year
Admission charged
At Fifth and Bennett Streets

Fifty-five trains departed daily from the former Midland Terminal Railroad depot, now housing the museum's main collection. Similar to an ant farm, a glass case shows how mines' multiple levels of tunnels and shafts overlapped and interconnected. Old-time slot machines and documents relate Cripple Creek's earlier casino days and Carry Nation's fervent anti-gambling crusade. Other buildings display assay equipment, photographs, and artifacts.

Pueblo
From its origins in 1842 as a trading post at the confluence of Fountain Creek and the Arkansas River, Pueblo evolved into an established city sustained by ranching and agriculture. Arrival of the railroad transformed it into a robust industrial center when, envisioning a Pittsburgh of the West, General Palmer founded the Colorado Fuel and Iron Company. Thousands of im-

Ludlow Memorial Monument

Ludlow Memorial Monument

Commemorating the Ludlow Massacre, this site (Interstate 25, exit 27, west 3/4 mile on dirt road) relates through interpretive panels the striking coal miners' demands and events leading to the infamous raid on a miners' tent settlement on April 20, 1914. What most outraged the public were the deaths of two women and 11 children who suffocated while hiding in a cellar below a blazing tent. An iron door currently covers the cellar entry.

Cripple Creek's First Millionaire

As a carpenter, Winfield Scott Stratton (1848-1902) beautified the woodwork of Colorado Springs' elegant houses with his signature notches and knobs. But history remembers him as the man who struck it rich in Poverty Gulch. Prospecting whenever time permitted, Stratton became captivated by rumors of Bob Womack's small gold discovery south of Pikes Peak. On the Fourth of July 1891, he staked his claim, appropriately named Independence. Within months, it elevated him from carpenter to Cripple Creek's first millionaire. Eight years later, Stratton sold the Independence for $10 million, reportedly the largest mining transaction to that time.

John A. Thatcher's fabulous mansion, now the Rosemount Museum.

migrants flocked to the jobs generated by rapid industrial development. By the turn of the 20th century, Pueblo's manufacturing output rivaled Denver's. Commemorating that era, the Union Avenue Historic District preserves late-1800s stone and brick buildings, now home to shops, restaurants and art galleries.

43. El Pueblo Museum
324 West First Street
(719) 583-0453
Open year-round Monday through Saturday
Admission charged
First and Grand Avenues

Located on the original trading post site, the facility presents the rich, multi-cultural heritage that sculpted lifestyles along this section of the Arkansas River. Exhibits profile key personalities, such as Jim Beckwourth who helped establish El Pueblo, and occupations from trapper to steelworker. New venues include a re-created 1840s trading post and a pavilion for observing archaeologists unearth artifacts.

44. Rosemount Museum
419 West 14th Street
(719) 545-5290
Open Tuesday through Sunday, closed January
Admission charged
Between Grand and Greenwood Avenues

John A. Thatcher, a powerful entrepreneur in cattle ranching, mining and agriculture, with controlling interests in more than 30 Colorado banks, moved his family into this 37-room, 24,000-square-foot mansion in 1893. The rhyolite-pink volcanic stone structure holds delicate beauty inside: ceiling frescoes, Tiffany chandeliers, lustrous golden oak paneling, silver door knobs, art glass windows and hand-painted murals. Guides enhance tours with details about the family and furnishings.

45. Pueblo County Historical Museum
The Vail Hotel
217 South Grand Ave.
(719) 543-6772
Open Tuesday to Saturday
Free
Union and Grand Avenues

From Pueblo's first piano to railroad memorabilia, the museum displays an eclectic collection that highlights precious slices of local life. A room brims with exquisite leather saddles crafted in Pueblo, once known as the

Intrepid Frontiersman

Born to a mulatto slave in Virginia and descendent of Irish aristocrats, James P. (Jim) Beckwourth (1800-1866) roamed the frontier as mountain man and trader. After working at Bent's Fort, in 1842 he founded his own trading post, El Pueblo, at the confluence of the Arkansas River and Fountain Creek. The post eventually evolved into the city of Pueblo. Married into three Indian tribes and adopted by the Crows, Beckwourth deeply respected Native Americans. Ironically, he led Colonel John M. Chivington to Sand Creek where troops slaughtered 150 Cheyenne and Arapaho. Horrified by the massacre, Beckwourth testified against Chivington.

James Beckwourth

Trails of Yesteryear

Guided westward by the Platte and Arkansas Rivers, mountain men trekked into Colorado in the early 1800s to trap beaver for their lucrative pelts. The pathways they created later became major transportation routes for stage lines, railroads and highways. In Colorado's northeast quadrant, members of the Rocky Mountain Fur Trade Company blazed the Colorado branch of the Overland Trail along the Platte River. To the south, the Cherokee Trail paralleled the Arkansas River to Pueblo, then cut north. Both of these routes connected with the Trapper's Trail, which stretched north-south from Laramie, Wyoming, to Taos, New Mexico. To profit from its brisk traffic, enterprising merchants built Fort Vasquez and similar trading posts. The most legendary of Colorado's early trade routes was the Mountain Route of the Santa Fe Trail. Following the Arkansas River west to bustling Bent's Fort, it then turned south through Trinidad and across Raton Pass to Santa Fe. For nearly 60 years, wagons teeming with millions of dollars of freight etched deep ruts which are still visible today.

Dazzled by the "Pikes Peak or Bust" promise of riches, 59er gold seekers followed former trapper routes to diggings in the Rocky Mountains. They also forged along the Republican and Smoky Hill Rivers, despite waters that often vanished into parched streambeds. North-south travel continued to flow on the Cherokee and Trappers Trails. The gold rush routes converged in Denver, Colorado City, Pueblo and other Front Range settlements. After replenishing their supplies, prospectors then trudged up steep, narrow canyon trails to mountain gold fields.

The first stagecoaches thundered into Denver from Leavenworth, Kansas, in 1859. Joggling on the Overland Trail, they followed the South Platte River, traversing the northeast quadrant of Colorado via Greeley and Fort St. Vrain. Farther south, the Smoky Hill Trail linked Atchinson, Kansas, with Denver. Dozens of stage line companies crisscrossed the plains, but only those that landed lucrative federal mail contracts survived any length of time. Stagecoach stops, such as Four Mile House, thrived as they provided lodging and meals for weary travelers.

Colorado's longest lived stage line, Barlow, Sanderson and Company, followed the Santa Fe Trail, using the ruins of Bent's Fort as a way station. Later it extended branches to Denver, Pueblo and deep into the San Juan Mountains mining region.

The importance of stage lines waned with the arrival of the railroad in 1870. Like their transportation predecessors, railways also followed many of the routes initially trod by the mountain men.

saddle makers capital. Also displayed is an 1880s *papier mâché* horse that once modeled products of the renowned Robert Frazier saddlery.

Cañon City

When the legislature offered Cañon City the option of a territorial prison or university, it chose the prison, a decision that has helped sustain its economy since 1871.

46. Museum of Colorado Prisons

201 N. 1st Street
(719) 269-3015
Open daily Memorial Day to Labor Day, Friday, Saturday and Sunday rest of year
Admission charged
First Street and Macon Avenue

Housed in the former women's correctional facility, the museum presents the history and evolution of Colorado prison systems. Each cell relates a singular theme, among them prisoner artwork, prison riots, cell furnishings, warden biographies and self-improvement programs.

Trinidad

After Don Felipe Baca established a prosperous sheep ranching business where the Santa Fe Trail met the Purgatoire River, he encouraged other New Mexican families to migrate north. Today, the Corazon de Trinidad National Historic District preserves the community's rich multi-cultural character as a major trail stop and livestock ranching center.

Santa Fe Trail traffic flowed in front of the Baca House.

47. Trinidad History Museum

300 East Main Street
(719) 846-7217
Open daily with guided tours May to October, by appointment other months
Admission charged
Between Chestnut and Walnut Streets

Bordering the Santa Fe Trail route, the museum complex comprises three entities, the Baca House, the Bloom Mansion and the Santa Fe Trail Museum, which relate life of the early inhabitants of southeastern Colorado. Located in former workers' quarters, the Santa Fe Trail Museum chronicles Trinidad's role in the trail's history. With photographs and memorabilia, it also profiles key leaders, such as Felipe Baca, a town founder and wealthy sheep rancher, and Casimiro Barela, a member of Colorado's Constitutional Convention and "the perpetual legislator" who championed Hispanic rights during his 41-year tenure.

Built in 1870, the Baca House represents the trail era. Wealthy rancher Felipe Baca bartered more than ten tons of wool for the residence. The two-story Territorial Style house combines adobe walls with such Greek Revival features as pediments over the windows. Period pieces portray the blending of Anglo and Mexican furnishings typical of a prosperous Hispanic-American family. For example, both an English-style fireplace, bordered by a book cupboard, and a lovely jerga, or hand-woven wool carpet, grace the family room.

In comparison, the neighboring Bloom Mansion, built in the 1880s, represents the railroad era. The Victorian home brims with ornate furnishings that rail transportation made more available.Topped with a belvedere, the stately Second Empire Style structure befitted the stature of its owner, cattle baron and banker Frank G. Bloom.

Santa Fe Trail

William Becknell's momentous trade expedition to Santa Fe in 1821 launched the Santa Fe Trail as a bustling commercial route. Spurred by tales of extraordinary profits, American merchants hastily set out on the 900-mile journey from Franklin, Missouri, while Mexican traders departed from Santa Fe. During the next 59 years, the dusty trail transported millions of dollars of merchandise.

Travelers faced a critical decision where the trail forked into two routes. Although 100 miles longer, the Mountain Route, proved safer than the Cimarron Cutoff. Following the Arkansas River westward, it turned southwest across the Comanche Grasslands to Trinidad and scaled Raton Pass, heading south to Santa Fe.

Several events favored travel over the Mountain Route. Bent's Fort, built in 1833, offered a supply station and safe haven. Three decades later, crossing Raton Pass became less arduous when "Uncle Dick" Wootton widened that segment of the trail. As railways advanced westward into Colorado, freighters opted to transport goods to and from New Mexico via trail and rail by traveling the Mountain Route to the railheads. That advantage waned as the railroad drew closer to Santa Fe. When locomotives steamed into the trail's western terminus in 1880, the era of the Santa Fe Trail ended.

48. Like an oasis, Bent's Fort provided travelers a haven in the "Great American Desert." Brothers William and Charles Bent and partner Céran St. Vrain established the trading post in 1833 to tap the surging commerce between the Missouri River and Santa Fe. During two decades, trappers, hunters, Plains Indians, Santa Fe Trail merchants and pioneers, and eventually American soldiers frequented the "Castle of the Plains." As many as 60 people were in residence at any given time. Laden with beaver pelts and buffalo robes, trappers and hunters swaggered into the trade room to barter. Arapaho, Cheyenne and other tribal members conducted peace talks in the council room. Mexican laborers maintained the fort. Seeking respite from the arduous Santa Fe Trail, travelers replenished supplies and repaired equipment. Indeed, the site epitomized a cultural as well as commercial crossroads. The trading post's role transformed during the Mexican War when it became a military staging point. When a cholera epidemic capped a series of tragic events, the fort was abandoned. Reconstructed in 1976, Bent's Old Fort National Historic Site [719-384-2596] depicts life at the trading post from 1833 to 1849 through costumed interpreters and historic reenactments.

Summit County / Vail Valley

High-altitude Breckenridge flourishes along the spectacular Ten Mile Range.

Nomadic Utes summered in this region's valleys, hunting bison, elk and other game. Then the 1859 gold rush invaded the peaceful terrain. Prospectors extended their search for the lustrous metal westward from Cherry Creek to the Blue River Valley and California Gulch.

While panning the Blue River, 59ers discovered the valley's rich placers. Soon, 50 miles of ditches and flumes conveyed water to diggings where, using water cannons, prospectors dislodged gold from the slopes. The new community of Breckenridge thrived on mining gold, first panning, then hard-rock mining, then dredging. A few miles away, the town of Frisco grew in the 1870s amidst gold and silver mines. Shortly thereafter, Leadville's silver boom rocketed incredible fortunes.

Farther west, the Gore River Valley yielded no gold or silver. But in the 1960s, another lucrative substance—snow—put it on the map when two mountaineers built a ski resort, Vail. The ski area's success set off another boom. Like the early prospectors, mountain towns that had lost their golden luster scrambled to reap potential fortune either by grooming their own ski resorts or by offering dining, lodging and support services. Today Vail enjoys international acclaim.

Frisco

Mountains dotted with gold and silver mines brought settlers to Frisco in the 1870s. Named after the town of San Francisco, it prospered until the end of World War I. Later, the lucrative ski industry revived its economy.

49. Frisco Historic Park
120 Main Street
(970) 668-3428
Open Tuesday through Saturday year-round, Sundays in summer
Free
Corner of Second and Main Streets

Left: Eagles Nest Wilderness Area soars above Vail Valley.

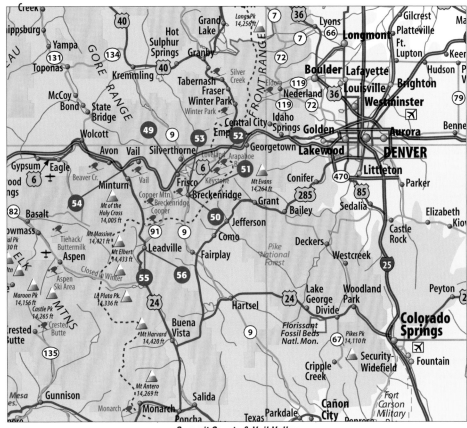

Summit County & Vail Valley

Photographs and artifacts inside the one-room schoolhouse museum chronicle Frisco's early days as a lively mining town. From a trapper's cabin to an 1890s city house, the park's relocated historic homes portray the evolution of mountain lifestyles. The site's eight buildings also include a log chapel and Frisco's first jail.

Breckenridge

Located on the Blue River between Peaks 7 and 10 of the Ten Mile Range, Breckenridge thrived on extracting gold from 1859 until World War II. Prospectors panned, placer mined, drilled rock shafts and dredged the river bottom in search of the precious ore. Wanting a post office, the savvy residents named their town Breckinridge, after President Buchanan's vice-president, but the town quickly changed the spelling when Breckinridge sided with the Confederacy. Now a year-round mountain resort, the village boasts a one-square-mile historic district whose false-fronted, wood frame buildings house attractive stores, restaurants and galleries.

50. Breckenridge Historic District Walking Tour, Briggle House and Milne Cabin

Rounds Building
137 South Main Street
(970) 453-9022
Tours Monday to Saturday, mid-June to September
Admission charged
In Blue River Plaza at Washington Avenue

Coursing along Main Street and into the residential district, a narrated tour guides visitors through the Alice G. Milne and W.H. Briggle houses, and highlights three phases of Breckenridge's development, starting with the hand-hewn cabins of early settlers in the 1860s. The Milne House exemplifies tongue-and-groove log house construction, chinked with horsehair and mud. Newspapers, mattress ticking and crating line the walls and ceiling for insulation. Main Street's wood-frame commercial buildings represent the 1880s mining phase. Besides providing greater signage, their second-story false fronts created a citified appearance. The post-1896 town phase evidenced more substantial construction. Banker William Briggle painted the trim on his house dollar-bill green and the clapboard real silver, which was

dirt-cheap after the 1893 silver crash. Simulating Italianate pressed tin, embossed paper embellishes the foyer walls. Items original to Breckenridge include hair art mounted in shadow boxes. Another family assembled a mail-order Sears & Roebuck house shipped complete with door knobs. Guides spice their narrations with stories about escaped slave Barney Ford, circuit preacher Father Dyer and naturalist Edwin Carter.

51. Edwin Carter Museum
111 North Ridge Street
(970) 453-9022
Tours Monday through Friday afternoons, mid-June through September
Admission charged
At Wellington Road

In this 1875 cabin, pioneer naturalist Edwin Carter stuffed and mounted Rocky Mountain birds and animals, including the black bear, lynx and ptarmigan currently on display. Wall-size photographs show the rooms crammed with specimens, reportedly as many as 3,300 at one time. Breckenridge memorabilia relate the local lifestyle at the time of his work.

52. Lomax Placer Gulch
Ski Hill Road
(Tickets at 309 North Main St.)
(970) 453-9022
Monday to Friday, mid-June through September, tour at 3 p.m.
Admission charged
Left side of Ski Hill Road beside Hunt Placer Inn.

From the 1860s to the 1880s, prospectors searched for gold nuggets and wires in Breckenridge's mineral-rich placer deposits

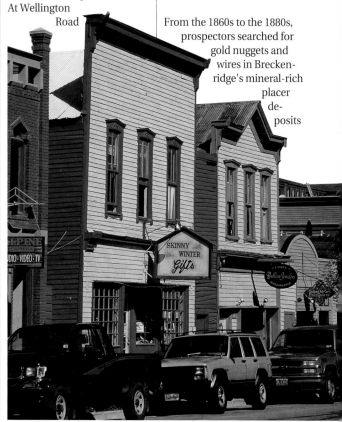

Historic falsefront buildings line Breckenridge's Main Street.

Breckenridge Walking Map

1. The Willoughby Cottage, 303 1/2 North Main Street

Young newlyweds spent the first months of their marriage in this small frame house—a remodeled horse stable.

2. Oren K. Gaymon House, 207 North Main Street

The editor and publisher of the Summit County Journal built this attractive Queen Anne cottage. Its distinctive details include spoon-carved doors, bay windows and cut-shingled gables.

3. Roby's Store, 101 South Main Street

This rare, wood-framed Italianate-style store specialized in groceries, provisions and miners' supplies for Breckenridge's early gold rushers.

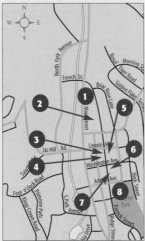

4. The Miner's Home Saloon, 123 South Main Street

Miners gathered here to play cards, drink liquor and swap news. The saloon's Western false front is a typical feature of most of Main Street's 1880s commercial buildings.

5. The Masonic Hall, 136 South Main Street

Patients climbed these stairs to the county physician's office until the fraternal order of Master Masons purchased the building in 1904. The order continues to meet at this location.

6. W. H. McDonald House, 204 South Main Street

A land surveyor built this tiny cottage. Later a female rancher purchased the house to reside in during visits to town.

7. The C. J. Enterlein House, 226 South Main Street

A grocer built this modern, seven-room house in 1898 for $1,450. Construction of similar family residences created a pleasant neighborhood.

8. The C.O. Lindquist House, 306 South Main Street

Embellished with elegant Queen Anne features, this two-story Victorian home was one of the largest and best-appointed residences on Main Street.

For 30 years, Father John L. Dyer (1812-1901) preached on circuits from California Gulch, now Leadville, deep into New Mexico. Shortly after arriving in Colorado, he became the presiding elder of the South Park District of the Methodist Church. At each settlement, he went from tent to cabin to store announcing the time and place of his sermon. To herald the start of the service, he blew a tin horn. He preached wherever people were gathered: saloons, shanties, barns, stores and miners' diggings. Because the collections that provided his remuneration were meager, he moonlighted as a mail carrier on the perilous route across 13,180-foot Mosquito Pass. In winter, he strapped on 11-foot-long home-made skis, which he called snow-shoes, and hauled some 25 pounds of mail by sled from Buckskin Joe to California Gulch. He also carried miners' sacks of gold, receiving a percentage of every $40-ounce he delivered. His heart, however, was in converting the souls of rugged miners, gamblers and adventurers. In 1879, Dyer purchased a lot in Breckenridge and gave half of the land to his congregation for the first Methodist church on the western slope of the Rockies. His church continues to serve the community.

Edwin Carter: Pioneer Naturalist

Edwin Carter and Edwin Carter Museum and interior.

When Edwin Carter [1830-1900] settled in Breckenridge in 1868, clear cutting of timber for mine shafts and houses denuded the slopes, destroying natural habitats. In addition, the chemicals used for ore extraction caused mutations in local fauna.

Appalled by the decimation of wildlife, Carter strove to collect one of each species of bird and animal. He hiked the mountain slopes and valleys for a quarter-century gathering some 10,000 specimens, including hundreds of sets of eggs.

Taking his meals at boarding houses, he kept much of his collection in his residence and welcomed the curious to visit his "museum" free of charge. Unlike traditional taxidermists, the naturalist posed the animals and stuffed them with dead grass impregnated with arsenic to keep bugs away.

Carter offered his entire collection to form a natural history museum in Denver, based on four conditions: formation of a corporation, construction of a fireproof museum building, receipt of $10,000 for the collection, and appointment as curator for life with a monthly salary of $150. When the means for financing a museum was resolved, his offer was accepted. What is now the Denver Museum of Nature and Science became incorporated in 1900.

by panning, sluicing sediment and washing away hillsides with hydraulic hoses. Lomax Placer Gulch, now serves as a museum where visitors learn about placer mining tools and techniques and how chemists assayed ore content. They can even try their hand at gold panning.

53. Washington Gold Mine
Illinois Gulch Road (County Road 518)
(Tickets at 309 North Main Street)
(970) 453-9022
Monday to Friday, mid-June through September; tour at 3 p.m.
Admission charged
On County Road 518 past its juncture with Boreas Pass Road

Deep inside this mine, men drilled and blasted walls of rock to extract gold-rich ore. Hard-hats in place, visitors follow ore-car tracks into the cool depths. Guides describe the hard rock mining process as they show miners' candles, dynamite, drills and other equipment.

Vail
The Gore River Valley slumbered during the gold rushes and well into the 20th century. When a state highway was built through the valley, a roadside village acquired the name Vail, in honor of state highway engineer Charlie Vail. In 1957, the small town's fortune improved when two World War II ski trooper veterans, Peter Seibert and Earl Eaton, set forth to build their dream—a ski area on Vail Mountain. After five years of

red tape and near financial ruin, their vision materialized. Vast bowls of snow soon became this valley's bonanza.

54. Colorado Ski Museum / Colorado Ski Hall of Fame
Vail Transportation Center
(970) 476-1876
Open Tuesday through Sunday. Closed May and October
Admission charged
On East Meadows Drive across from covered bridge into village

From the split pine log skis that 19th century trappers, miners and mail carriers used as transportation to today's high tech boards, the museum chronicles the evolution of ski equipment use and design. Exhibits of boots, bindings and skiwear of the past 130 years emphasize the efficiency and comfort current enthusiasts enjoy. One room honors World War II's courageous 10th Mountain Division ski troopers, several of whom pioneered Colorado's ski industry. The museum also includes the Colorado Ski Hall of Fame, displaying photographs and brief biographies describing inductees' contributions to skiing.

The Mountaineers

Two years of intensive training at Camp Hale, outside Leadville, honed the troopers of the Tenth Mountain Division into the elite outfit that shattered the German defenses in Italy in World War II. During rigorous training maneuvers, the mountaineers carried 80-pound packs while trudging through deep snow and climbing icy slopes in sub-zero weather. In combat, 14,300 troopers broke through the "Gothic Line" in the Italian Apennine mountains, leading to the unconditional surrender of the German forces there. The division suffered terrible casualties: 992 dead, some 4,000 wounded. The valor of individual mountaineers was honored with 279 Silver Stars and 2,810 Bronze Stars.

Top: Olympic medalist, Billy Kidd is honored at the Colorado Ski Museum / Colorado Ski Hall of Fame at Vail.

Leadville: Colorado's Silver Queen

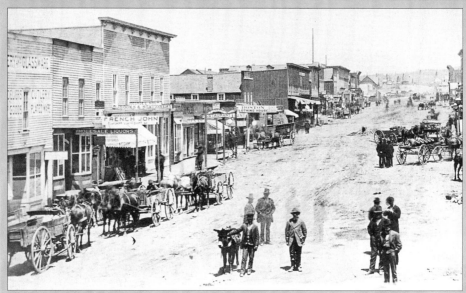

Rough and tumble Leadville as seen in this late 19th-century photograph of Harrison Avenue.

Gold lured the first prospectors to Leadville, but silver fashioned "kings." After fortune seekers panned and sluiced $5 million worth of gold out of California Gulch, all that remained was carbonate. The exorbitant cost of shipping ore to distant smelters made it unprofitable to mine. After analyzing the silver-lead ore, the St. Louis Smelting and Refining Company determined its rich silver content a worthy risk and established an on-site smelter. That action in 1877 launched the silver boom. Miners, smelter workers and investors stampeded to Cloud City, later named Leadville. Among them was Horace A.W. Tabor, a veteran prospector and storekeeper from neighboring Oro City. Grubstaking two prospectors who discovered the Little Pittsburg, Tabor reaped a fortune when the mine sold a year later for $1 million. His luck continued when he bought the

Chrysolite, despite the seller's deceptive salting of the shaft with stolen high grade ore. Tabor sank the shaft another 25 feet and struck silver ore that yielded $1.5 million. Smitten by lovely Elizabeth McCourt, known as Baby Doe, and abandoning his wife, Augusta, to marry her, the silver king created one of the era's greatest social scandals. With his wealth, he brought to Leadville such refinements as the Tabor Opera House, which helped offset the rowdiness of saloons and brothels. Audiences attended Oscar Wilde lectures, Houdini magic shows and Philip Sousa concerts.

The silver boom also turned J.J. Brown and his wife Margaret Tobin Brown into millionaires when their share in the Little Johnny reaped bountiful riches. The couple moved to Denver to take up residence among Capitol Hill's high society. Margaret later gained international renown as

"Unsinkable" Molly Brown, when, during the Titanic tragedy, she heroically helped other passengers survive. From 1879 to 1889, Leadville produced more than $82 million worth of silver. This fabulous era, however, crashed in 1893 when the US government repealed the Sherman Silver Purchase Act. The fortunes of Horace Tabor and other silver kings disintegrated overnight. After Tabor died, Baby Doe lived in poverty and seclusion in the one-room shack above Matchless Mine, where in 1935 she froze to death.

Today, Leadville's National Historic Landmark District preserves 70 square blocks of original Victorian-era buildings, including the Tabor Opera House. On the outskirts, roads wind past smelters' massive slag dumps and such early settlement sites as Oro City and Finn Town. Rickety cabins, hoist houses, shafts and

Leadville: Colorado's Silver Queen

other mining camp vestiges dot slopes and gulches. The Leadville Chamber of Commerce (719-486-3900) provides complimentary self-guided driving tour maps and other helpful information.

56. The National Mining Hall of Fame & Museum
120 West Ninth Street
(719) 486-1229
Open daily May through October, Monday through Friday November through April
Admission charged
Two blocks north of Harrison Avenue

Augusta Tabor

Horace Tabor

Baby Doe Tabor

55. Healy House and Dexter Cabin Museum
912 Harrison Avenue
(719) 486-0487
Open daily Memorial Day weekend through Labor Day, weekends in September
Admission charged
At 10th and Harrison

At the dawn of Leadville's silver boom, August Meyer opened the town's first ore sampler and smelting works. He and his wife entertained prominent citizens in this two-story wood frame house built in 1878. Named the Healy House after one of its later owners, the property brims with Victorian treasures donated by local residents, including a diamond dust mirror, a round alabaster table and an 1896 photo of the Leadville Ice Palace. Perhaps the most prized possession is a signature cloth whose embroidered autographs present a "Who's Who in Leadville." Built a year later, the Dexter Cabin looks like a typical miner's dwelling. Never a residence, it served as a private gathering place where flamboyant investor James V. Dexter hosted poker games for wealthy gentlemen. Oak and walnut flooring, exquisite wall coverings and elegant furnishings reflect his discriminating tastes.

Twelve rooms of memorabilia showcase mining methods and technologies employed across the nation. Specimens from significant gold discoveries in 17 states shimmer in the Gold Rush Room. The most dazzling—a 23-ounce gold nugget—was retrieved from the Little Johnny Mine, which turned J.J. and Molly Brown into millionaires. A series of 22 hand-carved wood dioramas depict Colorado's rich mining history. Other distinctive exhibits include a variety of scales for weighing precious metals, the Hall of Fame and a walk-through replica of an underground hardrock mine.

Index

Note: Boldface page numbers indicate main discussion of topic.

A

African Americans, 24
Allenspark, 10
Argo Gold Mill-Mine-Museum, 12, 45, **47**
Arrowhead Lodge, 10
Astor House Museum, 12, 27, **28**
attractions, 12–13
Avery, Franklin, 38
Avery House, 10, 12, **39**, **41**

B

Baca House, 11
Beckwourth, James, 8, 63
Bent, Charles and William, 67
Bent's Old Fort, 5, 8, 11, 12, 64, **66–67**
Black American West Museum & Heritage Center, 12, **24**
Black Hawk, 10, 45, **46**
Bloom Mansion, 11
Boulder, 6, 15, **30–33**
    map, 16
    Pearl Street walking tour, 32
    recommendations, 17
Boyington, L.C., 50
Breckenridge, 70–75
    walking tour, 12, 70–71, 72
Briggle House, 12, **70–71**
Broadmoor, 56
Brown, J.J., 11, 76, 77
Brown, Margaret Tobin (Molly), 6, **18**, 76, 77
Brown Palace Hotel, 19
Buffalo Bill Memorial Museum and Grave, 12, **30**
Byers-Evans House Museum, 12, **17**

C

Camp Hale, 11, 75
Cañon City, 6, **64**
Carter, Edwin, 71, 74
Casinos, 46

Centennial Village Museum, 12, 35, 36, **38**
Central City, 10, 45, **46**
Central City Opera House, 9, 10, **46**
Central Front Range, 45–51
    map, 46
    recommendations, 47
Chautauqua Park, 17, **33**
Clear Creek Canyon, 44, 45
Clear Creek History Park, 12, **29**
Cokedale, 11
Colorado History Museum, 12, **16–17**
Colorado Railroad Museum, 12, 17, **29**
Colorado Ski Museum/ Colorado Ski Hall of Fame, 12, 71, **75**
Colorado Springs, 6, 9, 53, **55–57**, 59
Colorado Springs Pioneers Museum, 12, **55–56**
Colorado State Capitol, 9, 12, 14, **17–18**
Coors Brewing Company, 27
Corazon de Trinidad National Historic District, 11, 64
Crawford, Dana, 19
Cripple Creek, 6, 53, **61–62**
    walking tour, 60
Cripple Creek District Museum, 12, 55, **62**

D

Denver, 6, 8, 9, **15–27**
    historic hotels, 19
    LoDo walking tour, 20–21
    map, 16
    recommendations, 17
Denver Museum of Nature and Science, 74
driving tours, 10–11
Dyer, John L., 73

E

Edgar Experimental Mine, 12, 47, **49**

Edwin Carter Museum, 12, 71, **74**
El Pueblo Museum, 6, 12, **63**
Enos Mills Cabin, 10, 12, **42**
Estes Park, 41
Estes Park Area Historical Museum, 10, 12, 36, **41**

F

Ford, Justina, 24
Fort Collins, 9, 35, **39–41**
Fort Collins Museum, 10, 11, 12, **39**
Fort Collins Old Town, 12, 36, 39
Fort Vasquez Museum, 12, **35–36**
Four Mile Historic Park, 12, **24–25**
Frisco, 69–70
Frisco Historic Park, 12, **69–70**, 71
Front Range
    driving tours, 10–11
    historic attractions, 12–13
    history, 5–9
    map, 13

G

Georgetown, 6, 44, 45, 47, **49–51**
    walking tour, 48
Georgetown Loop Railroad, 12, 47, **51**
Golden, 6, 8, 9, 15, **27–30**
Golden Pioneer Museum, 12, **28–29**
Greeley, 9, **36–38**
Greeley, Horace, 6, 37, 38

H

Hamill House Museum, 12, 47, 48, **50–51**
Healy House and Dexter Cabin Museum, 12, **77**
historic attractions, 12–13
history highlights, 8–9
Hiwan Homestead Museum, 12, **45–46**, 47
Hotel de Paris Museum, 12, 50, **51**

Index

I
Idaho Springs, 45, **47**, 49

J
Jacobs, Frances Wisebart, 17

L
La Veta, 11
Larimer Square, 12, **19–24**
Leadville, 6, 9, 11, **76–77**
Littleton Historical Museum, 12, 17, **26–27**
Lomax Placer Gulch, 12, **71**, 75
Longmont, 9, **38–39**
Longmount Museum, 12, **39**
Long's Peak, 8, 35
Love, Nat, 24
Lower Downtown Denver (LoDo), 12, **19–24**
Ludlow Massacre, 9, 62
Ludlow Memorial Monument, 62

M
MacGregor Ranch Museum, 12, 34, 36, **42**
Manitou Springs, 53, 55, **59**, 61
walking tour, 58
McAllister House Museum, 12, **56**, 59
Meeker Home Museum, 12, 36, **37–38**
Meeker, Nathan, 6, 9, **37**
Mills, Enos, 6, 10, **42**
Milne Cabin, 70–71
mineral springs, 59
Miramont Castle Museum, 12, 58, **61**
Mollie Kathleen Gold Mine, 11, 12, **62**
Molly Brown House, 12, 17, **18**
Mountain City Historic Park, 46
Museum of Colorado Prisons, 12, **64**

N
National Mining Hall of Fame and Museum, 12, **77**

National Western Stock Show, The, 25
Nederland, 10
Ninth Street Historic Park, 12, **18–19**
Northern Front Range, 35–43
map, 36
recommendations, 36

O
Old Colorado City, 8, **57**, **59**
Old Colorado City History Center, 12, **59**
Overland Trail, 64
Oxford Hotel, 19, 21

P
Palmer, William Jackson, 6, 9, 53, **55**
Pearl Street Historic District (Boulder), 12, **31–33**
Penrose, Spencer, 55, 56
Phantom Canyon Road, 10
Phoenix Gold Mine, 12, **47**, 49
Pike, Zebulon Montgomery, 5, 8, 53, **54**
Pikes Peak Cog Railway, 58, **61**
Pueblo, 9, **62–64**
Pueblo County Historical Museum, 12, **63–64**

R
railways, 28
cog, 58, 61
history, 6, 10, 15
museum, 29
narrow gauge, 51
Red Rocks Amphitheater, 31
Rock Ledge Ranch Historic Site, 7, 11, 12, 34, 52, **57**
Rocky Mountain National Park, 6, 10, **42**
rodeo (Greeley), 37
Rollinsville, 10
Rosemount Museum, 12, 55, **63**
Routt, John L., 9

S
Sand Creek Massacre, 6, 8, 63
Santa Fe Trail, 5, 8, **11**, 53, 64, **65**
scenic drives, 10–11
Silver Plume, 45, **49–50**
Southern Front Range, 53–67
map, 54
recommendations, 55
stampede (Greeley), 37
Stanley Hotel, 43
Stanley Steamer, 36, 41, 43
Stratton, Winfield Scott, 61, 62
Summit County, 69–77
map, 70
recommendations, 71

T
Tabor family, 6, **77**
Tenth Mountain Division Memorial, 11, **75**
trail routes, 5, 10–11, 64
Trinidad, 8, 9, **64–65**
Trinidad History Museum, 11, 12, 55, **65**

U
universities, 6, 9

V
Vail Valley, 69–77
map, 70
recommendations, 71
Vindicator Valley, 55, 61

W
walking tours
Breckenridge, 12, 70–71, 72
Cripple Creek, 60
Fort Collins, 40
Georgetown, 48
Lower Downtown Denver, 20–21
Manitou Springs, 58
Pearl Street (Boulder), 32
Washington Gold Mine, 12, **75**
Western Museum of Mining and Industry, 12, **56–57**
Womack, Bob, 6, 61

PHOTOGRAPHS

All photographs are by **David Muenker** with the following exceptions:

Historical photographs pages 18, 19, 20, 21, 30, 37, 38, 42, 54, 55, 63, 64, 74,76, and 77: Colorado Historical Society

Page 24, Nat Love: Black American West Museum

Page 38, Franklin Avery: Fort Collins Public Library

Nancy and David Muenker have explored the world as a travel writer/photographer team for 12 years. For most of their adult lives, Denver has been their home. Much like the '59ers, they individually set out for Colorado, seeking their personal fortunes. One summer evening, they met each other while walking their dogs in Washington Park. Shortly thereafter, they married and left company careers to pursue their passions for writing and photography. With cultural heritage as a predominant theme, their travel features appear in newspapers and magazines across North America.

They find Colorado's history fascinating. From rowdy prospectors to utopian colonists to perseverant conservationists, captivating characters have spiced development of the Front Range with rich, colorful themes.

"After writing this book," they emphasize, "we look at Colorado's expansive high plains and rugged mountains with even deeper respect and awe."